Quiet Talks with Earnest People in my Study

Spiritual Advice and Guidance from a Christian Minister

By Charles Edward Jefferson

Published by Pantianos Classics

ISBN-13: 978-1-78987-579-9

First published in 1898

Contents

Dedication v
How It Came About vi
I. The Unknown Man 9
II. The Maligned Man 11
III. The Misunderstood Man 14
IV. The Importance of Knowing Him 17
V. The Sermon 19
VI. What Is The Matter? 22
VII. Who Is To Blame? 24
VIII. Why Time Is Needed 27
IX. Vacation, and Why 29
X. Objections to Vacations 32
XI. Money 34
XII. Ministerial Liberty 37
XIII. Liberty Defined 39
XIV. Sympathy 42
XV. Co-operation 44
XVI. Considerateness 47

XVII. Thoughtlessness 49
XVIII. Ways of Killing a Sermon 52
XIX. Inspiring the Minister.. 55
XX. Appreciating the Minister 57
XXI. Criticising the Minister 60
XXII. Securing a Minister... 62
XXIII. Dismissing a Minister.. 65
XXIV. The Minister's Wife 67
XXV. The Mission of Laymen.. 69

Dedication

To The

𝕷𝖆𝖞𝖒𝖊𝖓 𝖔𝖋 𝕮𝖍𝖗𝖎𝖘𝖙𝖊𝖓𝖉𝖔𝖒

This Volume is Affectionately Dedicated
By a Minister
Who Esteems and Reveres Them.

How It Came About

Now that the talker has finished, let him tell you how he happened to begin. For more than ten years he was a layman. He has never recovered from it. Through all that period it never occurred to him that he should ever be a minister; and his habit of looking at things from a layman's standpoint became so deeply ingrained, that even to this day he often forgets he is a preacher and finds himself still thinking and feeling like a layman. He is more at home in a company of laymen than in a company of clergymen. During the years in which he sat in the pew he, like all laymen, supposed he understood ministers, and was capable of judging their work; and, like many laymen, he was sometimes harsh in his judgments, and unsparing in his criticisms. On entering the ministry he began to see things from another viewpoint. Mysteries once incomprehensible opened up in ways quite surprising. As a layman he had often wondered why so many preachers preached so poorly. As a preacher he began to marvel that preachers preach as well as they do. While an onlooker from the pew, the life of a minister seemed luxurious and free from drudgery; but in the pulpit it was borne in upon him that it is one thing to be a preacher of the Word, and quite another thing to be a hearer only.

Throughout his ministry he has listened with amused and profitable interest to the comments upon clergymen which laymen are in the habit of making, and has heard again and again many of the opinions and estimates which he had formerly held and expressed. One touch of nature makes all laymen kin. The misconceptions of a minister's work, and the misinterpretations of his conduct and speech, are often so ludicrous that it would seem incredible that intelligent people should be guilty of them were they not abiding and incontrovertible facts of current church history.

As the years have gone on he has found the conviction growing in him that one of the root causes of ecclesiastical disturbances is the chasm existing between the pulpit and the pew. A widening knowledge of church life, and the critical study of church quarrels, have forced him to the conclusion that it is not total depravity so much as partial ignorance which wrecks so many pastorates and leaves so many churches stranded. As a rule, unpleasantnesses in the Christian Church have sprung from very trifling matters, and in many cases there would have been no trouble had pastor and people known each other better.

Being convinced from experience and observation that peace and power in the churches can be deepened and extended by bringing pastors and peoples closer together, he resolved to throw open the doors of his study and invite the whole Christian world to come in. For just such confidential talks as it was in his heart to give, no place seemed so appropriate as his study. The pulpit was out of the question. Many themes and many people cannot be taken into the pulpit, but the minister's study is roomy and hospitable. In his library all ecclesiastical divisions and doctrinal differences sink into the background. Look at those shelves of books! Calvinist and Arminian, Jesuit and Puritan, Lutheran and Episcopalian, Baptist and Unitarian, Methodist and Presbyterian, heretical saints and orthodox martyrs, — all stand quietly together. A live preacher lives on them all. His people get them all in his sermons. There are at least two places on earth where denominational titles are lost sight of, and where ecclesiastical differences do not estrange, — a hymn-book and a clergyman's library. There is much talk nowadays about the desirability of Christian unity. It is comforting to believe that the Church is already one. Most of the differences which inflame and alarm do not go deeper than the skin. Christians are Christians, no matter what their denominational tag. Have you ever noticed that whenever Christians talk on vital themes they invariably slip into the same vocabulary and mood? The branches of Christendom differ in polity and definition, but they are all alike in their aims and needs. This is why the study-door was opened so wide.

But the door was not open for the admission of ministers. In all his talks the author has spoken only to laymen. This book is for them. Its ambition is to help them. The talks must be judged by their aim. If the frailties and shortcomings of clergymen are touched but lightly, or studiously ignored, it is not because the author is ignorant of them, or because he thinks it sacrilegious to lay them bare, but because ministerial delinquencies do not lie within the scope of his purpose. When he writes on the sins of clergymen it will require a larger book than this to hold what he has to say. If, on the other hand, he seems to bear down hard on the ignorance and perversity of laymen, it is not because he is blind to their excellences, or fails to measure the magnitude of their service, but because the aim of the talks is to call attention to those things in which laymen are most apt to go astray. The best people in the world, so the author thinks, are laymen. The tallest and sweetest saints whom it has been his privilege to know have been, not in the pulpit, but in the pew. There is probably no subject on which a true minister of Christ so loves to dwell in his thought as the sacrifices which laymen are making continually to advance God's kingdom. If the author had wished to tell what he thinks of the heroism and nobility and wisdom of the members of the churches, his talks would have filled a dozen volumes instead of one. If his estimate of laymen is unwarrantably exalted, the two churches which it has been his privilege to serve must be held responsible. Both of these churches have given him, in generous measure, all the things for which he pleads in the following pages. If the talks seem frank to the verge of bluntness, and if subjects often ostracized are discussed in language which is not minced, it is because the one who does the talking has been long convinced that laymen and clergymen have been and are too far apart; and that when pastor and people become willing to sit down together and talk about themselves, their wishes and purposes, with straightforward simplicity and unrestrained candor, the Church of God will enter upon an era of increased usefulness and power.

I. The Unknown Man

Certainly, come in! I am delighted to see you. Be seated, please.

And this is your first visit to a minister's study? I am surprised! The world as seen from a clergyman's study window is worth looking at, I assure you. You must come often.

You will pardon me, I hope, if I grow communicative, and even confidential. Your coming has so touched me that out of the abundance of my heart my mouth is sure to say things which I am not in the habit of saying in the pulpit.

You laymen, excuse me, do not call on the minister often enough. You have magnified the value of pastoral calling beyond reason. I wish that for the next few generations there might be a new emphasis on the "layman's" call. I have heard many church-members complain because the pastor had not called on them. I have never heard many confess that they had neglected the pastor. I shall consider this late call on me as fruit meet for repentance.

No one can look out upon the universal church without saying, "Something is wrong." Of course that is nothing new. There has always been something wrong, and probably there always will be. But it is the business of Christians to keep prying into the roots of wrong things that they may devise methods of setting the wrong things right. Let us examine a few of the roots.

The first thing which strikes one on even a hurried survey of the church is the widespread discontent. There are altogether too many dissatisfied parishes, and I am afraid there are just as many restless and hungry-hearted pastors. Church quarrels get into the papers with alarming frequency, and pastorates are distressingly short. Even where there is no noticeable friction, there is an appalling meagreness of energy and power. There is an immense difference between being well and not being ill. One may not know what health is, and yet never be sick. Many churches, not sick enough to quarrel with the minister, are, nevertheless, debilitated below the point at which effective work becomes possible. The wrangling, obstreperous churches are not so saddening, I think, as the shrivelled and impotent ones, which have only vitality sufficient to save themselves from extinction, and not vigor enough to show the world what robust and conquering Christianity is. One of the roots of all our church troubles, I take it, is the fact that clergymen and laymen do not come close enough together. Were I asked to give a recipe for lengthening pastorates and increasing the vitality of the churches, I should say, "Shorten the distance between the pulpit and the pew." Distance breeds misunderstandings. When pastor and people do not understand each other, the nerve of power and peace is severed.

I cannot help feeling that Protestants have an inclination nowadays to hold themselves aloof from their leaders. The eagerness with which the saints seize the back seats at prayer-meeting is significant because illustrative. The chasm of vacant pews to be seen in most churches between pastor and people is the visible sign of a spiritual gulf which ought to be bridged. The evils of mediaeval priestcraft have electrified the laity into a state of chronic repulsion; and the average Protestant seems to be afraid of being caught in the act of exhibiting too much reverence for a clergyman's office, or paying too much attention to what a clergyman says. The right to read and think for one's self is popularly construed to mean that everybody is as good a theologian as the minister. "The preacher is no longer an oracle! He has been hurled from his pedestal! He is a fallible mortal, no wiser or better than the people to whom he preaches! He labors under serious limitations, and has inbred and ineradicable biases, and therefore what he says must be taken with a grain of salt." The changes have been rung upon this strain until a multitude of professing Christians act upon the assumption that a preacher is to be endured but not heeded, criticised but not assisted, pitied and paid, but not honored and loved.

But nothing is gained by toppling a man from his pedestal unless this brings him closer to us. The important thing m this world is not to hurl men from their pedestals, but to understand them. And notwithstanding all we have heard about the dissipation of the atmosphere of mystery in which the "man of God" was once enshrouded, it is safe to say that the minister of to-day is but little better known than he was centuries ago. Once he was lost in the seclusion of the cloister, now he is lost in the press of the crowd. It is as easy to lose sight of a man in the dust as in the clouds. Although the clergyman of to-day is a man mingling constantly with men, no other man in the community is so imperfectly understood.

But you are not altogether to blame for not knowing him. You are busy, of course; I know that. His work is different from yours. He does it in solitude. And he never tells you about himself. If a clergyman talks about himself he is put down as an egotist. If he mentions his work in conversation he is talking "shop." He cannot complain. He cannot protest against injustice. He cannot explain himself or defend himself, or lay bare the secrets of his interior life; for Sundays are few, and on those days he must tell the people not of himself, but of One whom to know is life eternal.

The result is, the preacher is the unknown man of modern society. The world thinks it knows him, but it does not. The most that it says about him is erroneous. Dame Rumor repeats stories about his frailties and his idiosyncrasies, and jocose writers picture him in divers attitudes and colors, but he remains unknown.

I have often wished that preachers had time to talk now and then to their congregations a little about themselves. It would make them less professional, and more human to their people. It is singular no book has ever yet been written giving authentic glimpses of the ministerial world for the edification of laymen. Unnumbered volumes have been written by clergymen for the benefit of theological students, pointing out perils and burdens, and explaining methods and processes, and ministers are constantly telling one another of their experiences and needs; but little has been written or spoken for the purpose of letting laymen into the secrets and mysteries of ministerial activity and being. And herein the whole church suffers loss. Knowledge is essential to sympathy, and sympathy is indispensable to power; and power is the one thing which the church has been promised, and which it most conspicuously and lamentably lacks. We may expect a new Pentecost when laymen learn to put themselves into the minister's place. When we know each other better, some of the mists will roll away.

II. The Maligned Man

I was saying that the clergyman is the unknown man of modern society. Because unknown he is maligned. The world charges the clergyman with three cardinal sins, — laziness, covetousness, and cowardice. It suspects him of a half-dozen others, but it is sure of these three. To multitudes of men the minister is a gentleman of starched and elegant leisure, a lover of filthy lucre, a trimmer who cuts his discourses to fit his congregation. I suspect many Christians are not aware how vast are the areas of society in which this estimate is almost universally accepted.

That a clergyman should be considered a loafer is not strange. He does his work in solitude. Men see him as he rides in a carriage to marry a couple for a handsome fee, or as he offers remarks at a funeral, or as he speaks in the pulpit, or as he sits in a rocking-chair discussing the weather with some member of his flock, all of which the average man feels himself capable of performing without effort or fatigue. All other men — the farmer, the mechanic, the merchant, the builder — do their work where they can be seen of men; but the minister does his work in solitude. Not one of you ever saw a clergyman work. The harder he toils in secret, the more easily he preaches. This ease becomes added proof that preaching is to him as easy as breathing, and that therefore he does not work at all. His work, moreover, is mental. It is hard to convince hand workers that head workers really work. The perspiring farmer in the cornfield will not believe that the dainty artist at his easel beneath a tree is working. Nor can a mechanic readily believe that a man who reads books through the week and on Sunday exhorts people to be good has as hard a job as he has. It must needs be that to many men the clergyman should seem an idler.

Shall I shock you when I say that the clergyman belongs to the laboring classes, and that no man has a longer day than he? An eight or ten or even a twelve hour day would not be sufficient for his work. No mechanic in the country works as many hours a day as the faithful clergyman. Brain work cannot be done in the streets, and timed by the town clock, but it is work. The hardest work done in this world is brain work. Labor cannot be measured by the beads of sweat on the forehead. Work cannot be estimated in hours. It must be computed by expenditure of nervous energy, measured in ounces of vitality. The artist may pour out in a day more life on the canvas than the farmer on his cornfield. A man in writing a discourse can expend in three hours more nerve-force than a hodcarrier will expend in ten. In the higher moods of the mind, a single hour of creative work will leave a man sapless and limp. Never allow yourself to use the term "laboring classes" in referring to wage-earners. The expression is misleading, and perpetuates the ancient delusion that breaking down cells in the muscles is labor, while breaking down cells in the brain is play. Why should men who use their hands be considered laborers any more than teachers and doctors and lawyers and preachers? But this brain work is not all. There is heart work. The sweat of the heart has more blood in it than the sweat of the brow. To ride to a funeral is easy; but to bear daily the grief of wrecked homes — such labor bowed to the earth the Son of God himself.

It is because the minister is counted an idler that the world is so sensitive concerning his salary. It nettles men to see a man paid for doing nothing. The size of a minister's salary is always a matter of concern to the entire community. And it is a saying repeated with relish that a minister always feels called of the Lord to labor in the field which offers the largest financial returns.

That men should say this is to be expected. We always read others through ourselves. A man's heart is the lens through which he sees the world. The average man lives at the level of dollars and cents. How can he be expected to acknowledge that human nature can be swayed by motives higher than his own? A few facts are worth remembering. A clergyman has a divine right to compensation. He has, ordinarily, at least $15,000 invested in his head; and capital is entitled to some return. He is a laborer; and, as a workman, he is worthy of his meat. The vast majority of clergymen are underpaid. No other men do so much work for so little money as they. Brain commands higher prices in every other profession than in the ministry. That clergymen always rush to the church which pays best is false. A thousand clergymen in the United States can stand up and prove its falsity. The sneer which condemns a preacher for leaving a small church for a large one is both wicked and silly. A clergyman, unless providentially hindered, ought to accept the leadership of the largest church which he is capable of serving. Every man ought to enter the largest door which Providence opens in his face. Why condemn a minister for following the dictates of common sense, and for doing what is clearly a duty?

And is the average minister a trimmer? No! When you hear men say so, deny it. It is your duty to deny it, unless you know the assertion to be true. No one can injure the reputation of a clergyman without weakening the influence of the church universal, and hurting souls — it may be fatally. The world suffers more than you are apt to think every time a minister is vilified. "Then I and you and all of us" fall down, and earth's base seems to be built on stubble. If *your* minister, perchance, happens to be a trimmer, then work unceasingly to get him out of the pulpit. Do not simply talk. In God's name act! To laymen is committed no more important work than deposing ministers who are unworthy, and strengthening the arms of those who are true. There are more brave men in the pulpits of Christendom than in any army which ever followed a general to the mouths of the guns. To be sure, there is an occasional man who, like a coward, strikes only distant evils and sins which may be safely hit; but even in the apostolic band there was a man whose name was Judas.

III. The Misunderstood Man

A poet has suggested that much might be gained could we see ourselves as others see us; but the gain would be even greater if others could see us as we really are. It would from many a misconception free them. Oliver Wendell Holmes has called attention to the fact that in every conversation between two people there are six persons present. There is the first person as God sees him, as the second person sees him, and as he sees himself. There is the second person as God sees him, as the first person sees him, and as he sees himself. If this is true, there must be a regiment of ministers in every parish of a thousand people. Each member of the parish sees the minister at a different angle, and these thousand imaginary men form a nimbus around the real minister, concealing him from everybody but God alone. Just as Agassiz could form a fish from a single scale, so many persons have a fashion of constructing ministers from a splinter of a sermon, or a fragment of a course of action. An album containing a thousand portraits of himself as photographed on the minds of a thousand people would be an interesting volume for a pastor's library. It might humble him in the dust, but it would also bring consolation. If some of the portraits were black as Beelzebub, others would grace him with the glory of an archangel.

It is a current saying that clergymen do not understand people. Let us turn it round, and say that people do not understand clergymen. Why cannot a minister understand people? He works with human nature all the time. His library is stocked with books that analyze it, and discuss it in all its manifold varieties and operations. He is brought into closer contact with men than any other man in the community. He touches men on more sides of their nature. He hears death-bed revelations. He knows secrets which are intrusted to none other. He hears confessions of guilt and crime which do not get into the papers. He knows closets with skeletons in them of whose existence the community does not dream. He has an *entrée* into homes whose doors are shut to the world. He is with the sick, and the remorseful, and the poor, and the heartbroken. He listens to men's aspirations and doubts and fears, and complaints and anxieties, and loves and hates, and blasphemies and despairs. And yet he does not know human nature! It makes me smile to hear a business man say, in a supercilious tone, that preachers do not know people. This business man knows several church-members who do not pay their debts, and therefore the guileless minister would be very much surprised, if he only knew how many wolves in sheep's clothing are masquerading under his very nose — as though the clergyman does not know more of the hypocrisies and inconsistencies and unworthinesses of professing Christians than any merchant in the town! Ministers may seem innocent and *naïve*, but they know more of what is going on than the average man gives them credit for knowing.

I suppose they are counted ignorant of the world because on Sunday they do not manifest that sort of omniscience which the daily press displays. But a wise clergyman, knowing that his people through the week have had their minds stained and marred by the base and dismal, endeavors on Sunday to fix their hearts on things above. His refusal to go into the puddle does not prove his ignorance of it. Or is it because ministers do not indulge in the common vices of men? A man may know what is in men, and yet not accompany them in their sinning. Every clergyman has in him all the passions and powers by whose wrong use men become scapegraces and villains.

But this notion is overtopped in preposterousness by the idea that a clergyman has a better chance to be good than anybody else. The opinion is quite general among laymen. They ground their conviction on the fact that a minister is obliged by his calling to move in good society. Men hide their vices and curb their tongues in his presence. He need not touch anything unclean. He lives in his study and in the pulpit, and into neither place can the devil make his way. So it seems to many a layman. Many men are obliged to do their work among profane and foul-mouthed companions. Multiplied incitements to evil solicit them on every side. It is not strange that such men should look upon the clergyman as sheltered from the darts of the evil one, and as enjoying an immunity from temptation which is denied to all other mortals.

A minister on a pedestal has little influence over men. Unless he is in all points tempted like his brethren, he cannot be touched with the feeling of their infirmities. It is important, therefore, for laymen to remember that the battle of life is for all. Men may fight at different levels; but no matter where they stand, they are on a battlefield. Some sins are coarse and carnal, and others fine and subtle; but all alike separate the soul from God. There is no hedge around the minister. He has all the temptations of other men, and some additional of his own. The devil has access to his study. He was in Luther's study when the reformer threw his inkstand at him. He can ascend the pulpit stairs. He often does. What a host of demons the clergyman is obliged to meet and conquer! What opportunities for him to be a demagogue, a coward, a mischief-maker! How easy to pose as a defender of the faith, and cast insinuations on his brother minister who reads the gospel with a different emphasis! How easy to be vain of a fine voice or a superb presence! How easy to be envious of men just a little ahead of him in power and fame! How easy to be lazy, uncharitable, deceitful, domineering, autocratic, or peevish! How easy to wilt under discouragement! How easy to commit any of the sins to which our frail humanity is prone! The number of Christian ministers who in each generation have gone down the broad road while urging men to choose the narrow one is conclusive proof that clergymen, above all other men, need to put on the whole armor of God in order to stand against the wiles of the devil.

The fact that the minister deals constantly with spiritual things is proof to the unthinking that saintship to him comes easy, whereas the constant handling of high ideas and moral truths is a source of constant danger. Familiarity has a tendency to deaden sensibility; and just as soldiers often become blasphemous on the battlefield, and undertakers sometimes come to look on death without a trace of awe, so a minister, unless he prays and watches, will have at last a heart unresponsive to the very truth which he is sent to teach. It is something to be remembered always that the Scribes and Pharisees fell into a deeper ditch than did the publicans and harlots.

IV. The Importance of Knowing Him

Every layman believes that the minister should know his people. Every clergyman believes that too. All through his seminary course the importance of knowing his people, their names, dispositions, occupations, habits, and needs is dinned into him. Every minister who understands his business works constantly to establish a personal friendly relation between himself and his people. Without this relation his preaching comes to naught.

But it is equally important that a layman should know his pastor. It is not to be expected that the clergyman should go all the way. He cannot if he would. The distance between two souls is so great that while both together can bridge it, the bridging can be accomplished by neither one alone. If it is Christian and necessary for a minister to enter into the needs and experiences of his people, it is no less necessary and Christian that laymen should enter into the life and labors of their pastor. It is important for the layman himself. If he does not know his pastor, he cannot love him. If he does not love him, he will not be moulded by him. Love is the only flame hot enough to render the soul plastic. For the minister's sake also it is essential that his people should know him. His work is the building of men. He cannot transform men who are not responsive to his touch. And thus if laymen fail to understand their pastor, his efforts are nullified, the power of the church is crippled, and the progress of God's kingdom checked.

Let me suggest, then, brethren, that you get closer to the minister. Get as close to him as you can. In the church meetings get near him. The world condemns the clergy for poor speaking. The world forgets that the majority of ministers are obliged to speak under conditions which render effective speaking impossible. The most expert operator cannot send a telegram if the wire is cut, nor can the greatest orator speak with power if separated from his audience. Cultivate, I beseech you, a love for the front pews.

Get near him in your difficulties. The abuse of the confessional in the Roman Catholic Church has made Protestants shy of confession. But it should be borne in mind that it is the confessional, and not confession, against which Protestantism protests. The former is mischievous and dangerous, the latter is good for the soul. The confessional is built on a heaven-implanted instinct, — the instinct which prompts us to seek relief by sharing our sin or sorrow or perplexity with another. The institution would not have survived its monstrous abuse had not the instinct been deep-seated and ineradicable. Compulsory confession is tyranny, but voluntary personal conference is rational and Scriptural. Why not use your pastor more? A half-hour's conversation with him may bring you more relief than a score of sermons. Every life has its doubts and perplexities, its remorses and despondencies; and many a Christian flounders in darkness for years rather than let his pastor know that he is floundering. Many difficulties and doubts vanish in the light of larger knowledge, and all burdens are lightened when told to a friend. Make the pastor your friend.

Get close to him in his work. Seize his view-point. Grasp his plans. He will not command you, but he advises you. His advice ought to have in it something of the urgency and majesty of a command. Do not be afraid to obey him. Obedience is a virtue worth cultivating. There is none greater or rarer. The mediaeval doctrine of priestly authority we Protestants have discarded, but it was based upon a truth. In the New Testament the minister is given a place which we are just now in danger of denying him.

If you are close enough to him, you will not allow men to rehearse in your presence the stock yarns about clergymen which the world delights to repeat. Human nature is prone to act upon the principle, "From one learn all;" but never does it so act with such alacrity as when sitting in judgment upon ministers. A minister marries a rich wife, and almost immediately discovers that his throat is weak. Whereupon it becomes an adage that clergymen, like other men, loaf when they can. The son of a clergyman degenerates into a scapegrace; and in time that one boy becomes in the world's ears a million boys, and the lying remark that a minister's children are always the worst in the community hardens into imperishable tradition. An absent-minded, unpractical clerical bookworm fails to measure the value of money or the nature of men, and a story illustrative of the folly of the simpleton is published from Dan to Beersheba as an example of the ninnies and theorizers who have set themselves up as prophets in Israel. An indolent Reverend preaches old sermons, and jokes about his barrel which he keeps turning over; and his stupid joke is told wherever the gospel is preached, not so much as a memorial of him as a condemnation of the whole race of preachers. A clergyman is at the mercy of the community. If church-members do not defend him, who will? His reputation lies all exposed, and any one can injure it who chooses. A clergyman with a reputation spotted is impotent. His reputation is as important as his character. Other men can dispense with reputation, and do their work successfully. To the clergyman both reputation and character are indispensable. The farmer can sell his pigs and oats no matter what his neighbors say of him. The shrewd merchant can amass a fortune, even though a reputed libertine. The able lawyer can command an extensive practice, however rumor may busy herself with his name. But a clergyman cannot do his work if on his reputation there is a single stain. God is satisfied with character alone, but men are not. They demand reputation too. No matter how wise a clergyman may be, he can have little influence if supposed to be a dunce. No matter how saintly, his words are without weight if men suspect his piety. His influence is conditioned on the confidence and love of those to whom he ministers. To lie about him is to shut men's hearts against him. It was not from idle curiosity that Jesus asked the question, "Whom do men say that I am?" His influence over men depended not simply on what he was, but on men's estimate of him. And as soon as he found a man whose conception of him was adequate and true, he mounted at once into a great joy, and saw in vision a church against which the gates of Hades could not prevail.

V. The Sermon

I think I heard one of you say a little while ago that in your opinion the preaching of to-day does not come up to the demands of the times. I knew you would say that, and I agree with you. A great many ministers are just as certain of that as you are. It is not enough to say, as is often done, that the preaching of to-day is far superior to that of any preceding age. As a statement this is true, but as an argument it is fallacious. It does not cover the case. The vital question is. Has preaching in the last half century kept pace with the general advance in culture? And to this question the answer, I think, must be. No. That the average preaching in America to-day is far below the legitimate demand of the pews is, to my mind, a fact which cannot be successfully evaded.

You laymen, I imagine, are generally agreed that there is something wrong with the sermon. You find it difficult to say just what is lacking, but of the lack you are altogether certain. You do not agree among yourselves when you offer explanations, and I am afraid many of your explanations will not bear analysis. Some of you say that the cause of all the trouble is laziness, others say stupidity, others say profundity, others say otherworldliness, while still others of you confess that you are all at sea, and do not know how to diagnose a disease so complicated and distressing. You are sure of one thing, and that is that the culprit is the preacher.

It must be confessed that there are sluggards in the pulpit. But there would not be so many if the laymen did their duty, and drove these sluggards out. There is also an occasional minister who has not many convolutions in the gray matter of the brain. But these men constitute so small a minority of the modern army of preachers that we may drop them from our discussion, and pass on to consider the alleged sin of preaching sermons too profound.

When laymen fail to take an interest in their pastor's sermons, and try to follow his arguments in vain, they are sometimes generous enough to attribute their failure to their own stupidity and their pastor's extraordinary powers of thinking. It is comforting to many laymen to feel that their pastor's sermons are profound, even though the sermons fail to give them either light or strength. And occasionally a clergyman, doomed by his limitations to preach to a drowsy dozen, consoles himself with the delusion that it is nothing but the profundity of his thought which prevents the common people from listening to him gladly.

But no sermon ever fails because of its depth. The deep preachers whom nobody cares to hear are not deep at all. He is a shallow man who, commissioned to bear a message to the people, fails to speak that message in a language which the people can understand. A man capable of keen thought sees at once that it is his business to preach sermons which will feed and build up the men to whom he speaks. A preacher only dimly understood is no preacher at all. It is an awful condemnation on a preacher to say that his sermon is above the comprehension of the congregation to which it is delivered. No minister has ever yet been hampered by excessive profundity of thought. Many, however, have been handicapped by ignorance in the use of words. It is not excessive thought, but defective language, which puts people to sleep, and empties the pews. The plainest congregation can take in the greatest thoughts which the brainiest thinker can clothe in words. The sublimest conceptions can be expressed in homely sentences. The two profoundest preachers whom America has yet produced, Henry Ward Beecher and Phillips Brooks, were also the simplest in language, and the most easily understood.

Simplicity is one of the marks of greatness. So it has been from the beginning. Jesus of Nazareth, whose eyes pierced the depths, spoke always in familiar words, and never did he rise higher than when talking to an unlettered woman who gave him a drink at the well. What is taken for profundity of thought in the pulpit is often only technicality of language. The simplest thoughts may become obscure when couched in language which is cloudy. It is the misfortune of ministers that throughout their seminary course they read almost exclusively heavily Latinized English, and become addicted to the use of the dialect of criticism and the *patois* of philosophy. Unconsciously to himself a clergyman often drops the language of the home and the street, and speaks the language of the schools. Unless he keeps a sharp and constant eye upon his language, and reads with care the most human novelists and sweetest poets, he will find himself preaching in some other language than that wherein his congregation were born. There are no Pentecostal miracles unless preacher and people speak the same language. You are to be pitied, brethren, if your preacher preaches to you in the technical vocabulary of modern science or the cold and abstract phrases of metaphysics.

Nor are you correct when you say preachers are too doctrinal. Many are not doctrinal enough. It is doctrine which a preacher is ordained to preach. If he ceases to be doctrinal, his occupation is gone. The great doctrines of the Christian faith — such as the fatherhood of God, the deity of Christ, the presence and power of the Holy Spirit, the brotherhood of man, the forgiveness of sins, the judgment day, the life eternal — cannot be preached too frequently. Congregations fed on doctrines such as these have red blood and endurance. All others are scrawny and impotent. When you cry out against doctrinal preaching, you are using the wrong adjective. You mean to say that you do not like preaching which is metaphysical or speculative or scholastic. You have no taste for theories. You love truth. You are weary of speculations. You are hungry for facts. You do not want the guesses of men, but the doctrines of Jesus. You desire not only the sky ends but the earth ends of the gospel. And you ought to have them. Blessed are you if you have in your pulpit a man who can breathe easily the difficult air of the steep mountain-tops of spiritual experience, and who can tell you on the Lord's Day, in the sweet, familiar words of home, the things which he has seen and heard.

VI. What Is The Matter?

No, I have no objection to telling you what I conceive to be the radical defect in much of the preaching of our time. It is lack of spiritual passion. The tone of authority is faint. Too much of the preaching is like that of the Scribes. Clergymen are numerous, but prophets are few.

Here lies the trouble. Only a prophet can achieve genuine success in these hurried and fascinating days. Time was when a scholar could do it. When books were expensive, and locked up in the libraries of the *élite*, a man versed in book-lore could find a Sunday audience eager to listen to the information which he was willing to impart. Those days are gone. Before the rise of the daily paper, the preacher could be an editor, and make his sermons running commentaries on current events. That sort of preaching was once counted successful. It is a failure now. Before the multiplication of lecture platforms and music-halls and art-galleries, and other sources of intellectual entertainment and aesthetic gratification, fine music from the organ loft, and exquisite essays from the pulpit, seemed to satisfy all reasonable demands. But music, while it may still have charms to soothe the savage breast, is not conspicuously successful in attracting non-church-goers into the house of God. And much of the finest literary work displayed at present in American pulpits seems to be hopelessly lost on this unkempt and stiff-necked generation. Even the pulpit reformer does not wear his crown long. He has had his day, like the editor preacher and the rest. By striking one special evil hard, he may cause the world to resound for a season with the echoes of his blows, and may even succeed in chipping off a fragment of some false custom or established wrong; but unless a preacher is a great deal more than a reformer, he cannot long hold the attention of an intelligent congregation, or hope to build an enduring Christian church. In short, the poor preacher has been ousted from the snug position of editor, lecturer, essayist, reformer; and there is nothing left him now but the arduous vocation of a prophet.

And this has been his true place from the beginning. His other positions were either usurped or thrust upon him by the exigencies of the times.

The printing-press has pushed him up at last into his proper sphere. If he attempts now to compete with other men in their fields of labor, he invites the failure which he deserves. The position of a minister is unique. His mission is momentous. His work, while fitting into the labors of all other servants of the Lord, is different from theirs. The moment he forsakes the task appointed him, and attempts to share the work and honors of other men, swift retribution follows in his track. Woe to the preacher who in these modern days shirks the wrestlings and agonies of the prophet, and attempts to perform the duties assigned to others!

And yet this is the very thing which many preachers are doing. Notwithstanding the discussion *ad nauseam* through the week in the daily press of every happening and event, there are preachers who have the temerity to expect people to come to the church on the Lord's Day to hear the old newspaper straw threshed over again. And notwithstanding every centre-table groans with periodicals and magazines edited with consummate ability, and filled with articles written in many cases by the pen of genius, there are ministers who dabble on the Lord's Day in literary discussion and philosophical speculation, and then wonder why the blessing of the Almighty does not rest upon their labors. There is an itch abroad just now to work reforms. Everything is being overhauled, from systems of theology to boards of aldermen. The social order is rotten, the industrial system is accursed, the ecclesiastical *régime* is ripe for burning — so men assert. There is a hubbub of discordant voices, each voice screaming out a panacea, and promising the golden age; and in this fury for readjustment and reconstruction, too many pulpits, I am inclined to think, waste their time and strength. It is a proof of Christ's matchless greatness that he stood in the presence of the Roman Empire and never struck it. His work was to strike the heart. By striking the hearts of peasants, he overturned the empire. He says to his heralds, "Follow me!"

Unless a sermon is different from all other forms of address, the world to-day does not care to hear it. If tired men and women are to be expected to attend public worship Sunday morning, the atmosphere of the house of God must be made different from that which these people breathe through the week. The late R. H. Hutton, in one of his essays, says that Walter Bagehot once asked him to hear one of the afternoon sermons of the chaplain of Lincoln's Inn, Frederick D. Maurice. Bagehot assured Hutton that he would feel that something different went on there from that which went on in an ordinary church or chapel service, that there was a sense of "something religious" in the air which was not to be found elsewhere. Bagehot's word was fulfilled. Hutton heard and saw and felt that day things which lived in his memory through life. He heard a prophet. Maurice spoke for God. The intense and thrilling tones, the pathetic emphasis, the passionate trust, the burning exultation, the atmosphere of reverence and devotion, awed and subdued the worshippers. The church became indeed a holy place. The words of the service seemed put into the preacher's mouth, "while ne, with his whole soul bent on their wonderful drift, uttered them as an awe-struck but thankful envoy tells the tale of danger and deliverance."

It is this "something religious" which one misses in too many of our American churches and in too much of our modern preaching. Bright things, true things, helpful things, are said in abundance, but the spiritual passion is lacking. The service smacks of time and not of eternity. The atmosphere of the sermon is not that of Mount Sinai or Mount Calvary, but that of the professor's room or the sanctum of the editor. The intellect is instructed, the emotions are touched, but the conscience is not stirred, nor is the will compelled to appear before the judgment throne and render its decision. The old tone of the "Thus saith the Lord" of the Hebrew prophets is lacking. Men are everywhere hungering and waiting for it, but in many churches they have thus far waited for it in vain.

VII. Who Is To Blame?

Nor is the minister altogether to blame. He is the victim of circumstances and the *Zeitgeist* and — laymen. The time was when people lived largely in villages. In those rural days the minister was preacher and teacher, and pastor and administrator, and counsellor and general public servant. The world to-day lives largely in cities, and it is the carrying of rural traditions into city conditions which is in part responsible for the present dearth of strong preaching. It is the old, old story of laying aside the commandment of God and holding the tradition of men.

In village days every man was expected to be able to do a dozen different things, and the preacher was not an exception to the rule. The farmer understood a dozen different trades, and why should not a clergyman fill a dozen different positions? But

> New occasions teach new duties;
> Time makes ancient good uncouth.

The village has developed into a city, and all the problems have changed. The process of specialization has gone steadily forward, by which each man is given some one specific thing to do. Each department of work is divided and subdivided indefinitely, thus securing greater concentration and an increase of efficiency. The expert lawyer masters only one province of law, the expert physician confines himself to one class of diseases, the expert editor writes on only one line of subjects, the expert teacher teaches only the fragment of one branch of knowledge; but the minister is still expected to preach, and at the same time do a hundred other things. The work connected with the average city church is sufficient to fill the time and exhaust the energy of several men, but in the majority of cases the minister is left to bear all the burdens alone. He must be the director of the church's manifold activities; he must make pastoral calls, after the fashion of his country ancestor; he must be public servant, answering letters innumerable, speaking at banquets, serving on committees, presiding at meetings, acting as director or trustee of colleges and societies, orating at anniversaries, pushing forward lagging reforms, encouraging numberless enterprises; and then, fagged in body and jaded in mind, he goes into the pulpit to preach! And you laymen — some of you — wonder why preachers preach no better than they do! The wonder is that we can preach at all. The average preacher is simply sapped and overwhelmed by the avalanche of demands which the modern world makes upon him.

The spirit of the age — Matthew Arnold's *Zeitgeist* — comes in to make matters still worse. A mania for organization has seized the world. The distemper has penetrated the life of the churches. The average church boasts more societies and meetings than an industrious rosebush displays roses in June. In this fury for organization, the life of many a church is being ruthlessly dissipated. So much time and energy are expended in keeping the ponderous and complex machinery in motion that healthy Christian life is sacrificed, and effective work becomes well-nigh impossible. The church suffers, the home suffers, weary mortals suffer — especially the minister. He finds himself the business manager of a large concern. He must keep his eye on all sorts of societies, clubs, and guilds. He must attend the meetings of these at stated intervals or be suspicioned of lukewarmness in the Master's cause. The modern church may win applause by multiplying its agencies for serving men, but all such apparent progress is dearly paid for when secured at the expense of the preacher. A boys' brigade drill or a soup-kitchen or a gymnasium will never do the work of a searching and inspiring sermon. The word of the Lord coming hot and strong from prophetic lips is the one thing which the church can never dispense with without forfeiting her life. Anything — no matter how excellent in itself — will in the long run, if it diminishes the power of the preacher, cripple the efficiency and retard the progress of the church. It is not by philanthropic agencies nor the creation of new societies, but by the "foolishness of preaching," that the world is to be redeemed.

Therefore, brethren, guard your minister with all diligence, for out of his heart proceeds the word of life. If you convert him into an errand-boy or a packhorse, you not only kill him, but you check the progress of the kingdom. If you permit him to fritter away his time on organizations, and squander his strength in administration, he cannot speak to you on the Lord's Day with an energy that will stir you, and with a knowledge that will build you up. There is nothing more pathetic in the religious history of America than the cruel way in which ministers are sacrificed to the ignorance and thoughtlessness of Christians. One layman by himself is not cruel; but five hundred or a thousand laymen, when banded together in a Christian church, can do things which a savage would blush at. They can sacrifice without compunction the health and growth and domestic life and usefulness of their pastor, and finally leave him a wreck. Much is said about the dead line, and clergymen are roundly condemned for reaching it. A minister must inevitably reach it, and early too, if he does not have sufficient will-power to resist with dogged pertinacity and martyr-like heroism the encroachments on his time and energy which good-hearted but inconsiderate people are sure to make. Many a faithful servant of the Lord has in early life, in order to meet the voracious demands of his parish, cut short his hours for study and for prayer, and then been subjected to the galling humiliation later on of hearing from the lips of the very persons whose foolishness had undone him, the damning assertion, "He is a very good man, but he does not hold the people!"

Let your minister preach. When he tells you what hours he needs for study, let him have them. If he does not call so frequently as his predecessor, say nothing. Measure him not by the number of door-bells he rings, but by the impulse he gives the community toward God. When he is absent from some occasion which you wished might have been graced by his presence, do not complain or condemn. When he declines to say "yes" to your every invitation, remember that you are only one of a thousand persons who have a claim on him, and that ministers have rights which laymen ought to respect. When ministers do less they will do better, and when churches demand less they will receive more.

VIII. Why Time Is Needed

I know how a layman looks at it. He thinks that a minister can begin Monday morning to write his sermons, and can write straight on till Saturday night. With a clean sweep of six long days at his disposal, what more can a reasonable man demand? But it should be remembered that according to God's law a man must drop his work one day in seven. The clergyman who does not do this pays the penalty like any other transgressor of the law. Moreover, few clergymen have more than their mornings in their study. The afternoons are filled with parish duties, and the evenings with social functions and religious meetings. Thus the vast week dwindles down to five short mornings in which two sermons must be prepared. And as if even this were too much, frequently a funeral or some other imperative call steals away one of these five precious mornings.

Within these narrow hours what tremendous work must be done! It is a popular notion that the preacher's hardest work is the writing of his sermons. His most arduous labor is preparing, not his sermons, but himself. Any one can write down a sermon after he has the sermon in him; but to get one's soul into that mood in which sermons blossom, to lift one's self to those high altitudes at which the word of God is audible, ah, there's the rub! What study! What meditation! What prayer! A sermon is not a thing that can be dashed off at any moment and without heart-strain. A sermon grows. Growth requires time. A sermon eats up the life-blood of a man. To keep the fountains of his life from running dry is the minister's most critical problem. He must be an indefatigable worker. Intellectual treasures from every quarter must be swept into his mind by reading, wide and constant. He must be a student. He must dig deep in the mines of thought, and wrestle with the problems which distress the age and the ages. He must meditate. He must have time to keep still that great thoughts may take shape in him, that opinions may crystallize into convictions, and that dim truths may become clear. He must pray. He must continue long in prayer.

No man can pray in a hurry, or meditate in haste, or study with a hundred duties standing at the door and shouting at him. But the modern preacher has little time. He goes through the week on a hop, skip, and jump. He is in a constant flurry to meet his next engagement. He is a Martha busied about many things. The better part has been taken from him. A thousand odds and ends of parish work keep him in a frenzy of activity, which saps the springs of intellectual energy and spiritual life.

Brethren, we have now reached the root of one of the great problems of our day. The various distressing pulpit phenomena, which we all lament, and whose correction seems to be beyond our skill, can nearly all be traced, I think, to the crowded and feverish life which a modern minister is obliged to live.

It is lack of time which drives so many preachers to palm off editorials as sermons. There is a vast difference between an editorial and a sermon. The former is an opinion, a comment, a discussion of a problem. It may be written without emotion, and oftentimes in haste. The sermon, like a poem, is a creation of the spirit, and comes into existence only through an experience which melts and transfigures the heart. Editorials may be written in the street; sermons come to the soul only at high levels. The minister must, like Moses, go up into the mountain alone.

It is lack of time which is cutting pastorates short. Preaching becomes thin, and laymen rebel. Preaching is thin because preachers are thin. Preachers are worn thin by endless activity. A man, to keep intellectually robust and spiritually rich, must have leisure for contemplation and wide study. Pastorates are becoming short, not because preachers are lazy, but because they are so busy in doing things that they preach themselves empty in three or four years. Many a minister's lamp goes out simply because he has no time to supply himself with oil.

It is lack of time which is partly responsible for the increased demand for evangelists, and for the numerous cheap devices adopted by preachers for wheedling men into church attendance. If preachers do not have time to read great books and assimilate great ideas, it is not surprising they should fall back on pictures and choirs, and call in as often as possible an outsider to lighten the drudgery of their sermonic work. The increased dependence on travelling preachers is, in my judgment, one of the most ominous and deplorable signs of the times.

And how shall we account for the absence of that fire without which preaching is vain? A sermon is nothing unless touched with emotion. Emotion cannot be manufactured. It is the result of meditation. The Psalmist says, "While I mused, the fire burned." Without musing there is no burning. James Russell Lowell, in one of his letters, says, "My brain requires a long brooding-time ere it can hatch anything. As soon as the life comes into the thing, it is quick enough in chipping the shell." From London he wrote to a friend, "I am piecemealed here with so many things to do that I cannot get a moment to brood over anything as it must be brooded over if it is to have wings. It is as if a sitting hen should have to mind the door-bell." That is the experience of the preacher. He is piecemealed. He is the victim of the door-bell. He cannot hatch his thoughts fairly out as he goes along. Little opportunity is given his nature to kindle into flame.

If preachers are to speak for God they must be given time to find out what God says. The words of John the Baptist rolled out upon his hearers like molten lava because he had brooded so long over the soul's need and God's will that when he emerged from the desert there was a fire burning in the marrow of his bones. Jesus in the quiet of Nazareth meditated and mused through the years until he was caught up by a spirit which carried him from the shop to the cross. No wonder he spoke as one having authority, and that men wondered at the words of grace which proceeded out of his mouth. And throughout his short public life he again and again turned his back on men in order to be alone.

IX. Vacation, and Why

A vacation for a minister is not a luxury, but a necessity. Of course a man may preach every Sunday for years; but if a man is to preach at his best, he must have annual periods of rest. If through mistaken zeal a clergyman declines to take a vacation, his church should stoutly insist on his obeying the laws of psychical health. If through carelessness or ignorance a church fails to provide for an annual vacation, the minister should take it anyhow. No servant of the Lord should ever allow himself to be robbed by any company of men of the conditions essential to largest usefulness and power.

A vacation is as necessary for the rural clergyman as for his brother in the city, but for different reasons. The village deadens, the city exhausts. The foe of the rural minister is rust; the enemy of the city minister is mental and spiritual dissipation. A thousand influences play on the minister in the city to keep him alive. He is in danger of dying of excess of life. In the hamlet the minister is himself the fountain of life. He is the magnetic battery from which every enterprise must be charged. His mission is to quicken and arouse. But in order to stimulate others, one must himself be stimulated. Every village pastor should, if possible, spend at least one month of every year away from his parish. His people ought to insist on his doing this. He should make an annual pilgrimage to some intellectual centre. He will bring back in new impressions and fresh ideas more than enough to compensate the community a hundredfold for all that his vacation has cost. Who can walk through the drowsy streets of the ordinary village without appreciating the magnitude of the task laid upon the country parson of keeping enthusiasm intense and thought-horizons wide?

The city pastor must have a vacation to keep his nature from wearing thin. The endless round of engagements, the enormous correspondence, the awful burden of poverty and woe, the constant drain on the centres of vitality, render unceasing work dangerous, if not fatal. Even if a man were physically strong enough to stride through the months without a pause, the nature of the mind is such that unceasing sermonic activity is fatal to highest pulpit power. A preacher is a teacher. A teacher's worth is measured by his ability to inspire. Inspiration is conditioned on vitality and vigor of the creative faculties of the mind. A preacher must create impulse. A jaded preacher is no preacher at all. The man in the pulpit must give forth life. The more life he radiates, the greater his service to the world. Truth must in him become incarnate, and burn with a flame which fascinates and transforms. No man can teach even language or science with highest efficiency straight through all the months of the year. Universities make no mistake in granting professors long annual vacations, and in giving them one complete year in seven. Without opportunities to recuperate and blossom, the teacher degenerates into a hack, a machine, a pedant. Much more necessary is periodic rest to the man who deals, not simply with the intellect, but with the affections and the will. To cleanse and stir life at its fountain-head requires a man intensely human, and in every fibre of his soul alive. Human nerves are not steel. If always stretched, they deteriorate or break. A preacher must be a thinker. He ought to think closely, consecutively, accurately. Only a fresh mind thinks truly. A fagged mind cannot be trusted. A wearied preacher tires his congregation. He does worse, — he misleads. He does not see things in their right relations, and cannot present them in their true proportions. A man may exhort or retail anecdotes everlastingly, but that is not preaching.

More than the preacher's intellect is in danger. His spiritual life is at stake. It is possible to work for God until all sense of God is lost. An overworked preacher finds himself asking with Pontius Pilate, "What is truth?" The eclipses of faith, alarmingly frequent in the ministry, are largely the result of overwork. A clergyman must get away occasionally from the Bible. He must touch God in the sea and sky and woods. He must listen, not always to Hebrew prophets, but sometimes to American frogs and katydids and birds. He must drop the idea of saving others, and be still that God may save him. In the months of work he must be self-assertive. His aim is to impress men. He hurls himself upon them. He looks for results. This mood, if never broken, becomes destructive of the higher life of the soul. There is nothing more pathetic than the degeneration which often goes on in the character of men ordained to preach the gospel. As the years go on the temper loses its sweetness, the disposition becomes autocratic or peevish, the mind is sicklied o'er with a morbid cast of thought, the very structure of the soul seems in some cases to crumble into hopeless decay. Many a minister, whose head is full of foolish fears and whose sermons are weighted with morbid fancies, would be born again if he could spend a few months under the trees or on the sea. Anything which will widen the minister s outlook, elevate his ideals, cool the fever of his nerves, quicken his impulses, and restore the balance of his judgment, ought to be sought after by a congregation as rubies and fine gold.

Indeed, it is for the sake of the people rather than for the sake of the preacher that a vacation is necessary. A church whose pastor takes no vacation is of all churches most miserable. It does a church good to escape occasionally from the man who is its head. It is not best for a congregation to listen continuously to the same man, no matter how wise or good he may be. It is of vast advantage for laymen to sit at the feet of men who see truth at different angles, and who enter hearts by different avenues of approach. A voice, no matter how sweet, loses its edge if heard too often, and fails to reach the heart as a voice does whose accent is fresh, and whose intonations have in them the charm of unfamiliar music. A church is roused to new intellectual alertness, and lifted to higher levels of spiritual vision, by listening now and then to voices that are new. For his people's sake, as well as for his own, no minister can afford to stand in his pulpit every Sunday in the year.

X. Objections to Vacations

I think one of you remarked a little while ago that the devil never takes a vacation. The tone in which you said it compelled an inference and outlined an argument. But the argument rests on two erroneous suppositions. It is not true, as is sometimes assumed, that a clergyman is under obligation to follow the example of the devil, nor is it true that a community is completely at the mercy of his Satanic majesty the moment the minister goes out of town. If the devil can in one month undo all the work which the minister has done in eleven months, the loss is not so great as you imagine. Such work as that ought to be done over again. It is only when men build of hay and stubble that their work goes up in smoke under an August sun. Church-members who live and work like Christians only when the minister's eye is on them are not sufficiently Christianized to stand the test of the judgment day. The minister is not the church, and it is foolish to take it for granted that if he is absent the church of God practically ceases to be.

You say that many churches are too poor to afford the luxury of a summer supply. What of it? A summer supply can be dispensed with. There are forms of church service other than the preaching service. A praise or prayer or Bible study or conference service, or a service copied after the model set us by the apostolic church, in which each Christian had a Psalm or a doctrine or a tongue or a revelation or an interpretation, is as legitimate and Scriptural as a service in which the minister does it all. If you feel your church cannot survive a month without a weekly sermon, then why not have the four best readers in the church read in turn sermons from four modern pulpit princes? Such an innovation might prove as refreshing as the dew of Hermon.

Ah, I have not struck the difficulty yet? It is the pastoral work that cannot be neglected. Of course not! But it is an error to suppose that only a clergyman can do pastoral work. Every Christian is by divine appointment a pastor, and it is of the essence of the Christian life to shepherd some of the Master's sheep. Laymen when living up to their privileges are pastors, and are abundantly able to pray with the sick, assist the poor, advise the perplexed, and comfort the dying. If the church has no members except the pastor who are able and willing to do this, it is high time for that church to put on sackcloth, and confess that it is wretched and miserable, and poor and blind and naked. But you say sick people prefer the pastor. Suppose they do. Some sick people have a habit of preferring a lot of things which -are unreasonable, and which it is not best for them to have. Persons when sick have no more right to be selfish than other folks, and should learn the high art of sacrificing their preferences and likings to the welfare of others.

But how about the dying and the dead? Surely a clergyman is indispensable in such cases! Not at all. A Roman Catholic can go into heaven without extreme unction, and there is no reason why a Protestant should not die in peace without a pastor's prayers in his ears. Moreover, a clergyman is not indispensable at a funeral. No clergyman officiated at a funeral in New England for more than a half century after the landing of the Pilgrims. Neither the living nor the dead, so far as can be ascertained, suffered from this singular procedure. The clerical custom of conducting funeral services is an innovation. Jesus never did it. He did not lay it down as one of the duties of his apostles. Neither the twelve nor the seventy were instructed to bury the dead. If Paul had ever been twitted on being out of town when some Christian saint needed burial, he would no doubt have replied with swift alacrity, "Christ sent me not to attend funerals, but to preach the gospel!" If ministers of the Lord need a vacation, surely dead people must not be allowed to block up the way. That church is poor indeed in which there is no layman worthy and able to offer a prayer above a casket, or repeat "dust to dust" beside a grave.

A minister's vacation should not be less than a month. A two weeks' vacation is no vacation at all. A clergyman cannot drop his work as a clerk drops his yardstick or a bookkeeper his ledger. The minister's burden is spiritual. It is not easily shaken off. It wears down into the fibre of the soul. Deliverance comes only in time. At least a week is needed for working one's self out of the sermonic mood; and if at the end of this first week the preacher must begin to work out new sermons for the coming Sunday, his vacation practically amounts to nothing.

In many cases one month's rest in twelve is not sufficient. The time demanded depends on the man and the parish. Tough and callous men, who radiate little energy, require less vacation than men of sensitive nature and vast genius for expending life. It is cruel to expect equal things of all men. Dray horses and race horses demand different treatment. One man will burn up more life in one sermon than another will burn up in twenty. To give the first man no more vacation than the second is both foolish and wicked. The coarse-fibred and lethargic man may boast that he never takes a vacation; but if he were more finely conscientious in his work, and more tremblingly alive in body, mind, and spirit, he would suffer the same exhaustion which overtakes his fine-grained and passionate brother. And parishes differ in their demands. When parochial duties are multitudinous and pulpit work is unusually exacting, a vacation of two or even three months is not unreasonably long. Ministers with extended Vacations do not spend all their days in idleness. In the vacation months they store up food with which to feed their people through another year. By travel or by study and long, uninterrupted meditation they freshen the spirit and enlarge the heart that those whom the Lord has given them may enjoy a richer ministry at their hands. Study your minister, brethren, his temperament and constitution. Measure his strength, and the tax which his work levies on it, and then, paying no attention to what other churches are doing, give him all the time for rest he needs.

XI. Money

Money is my theme. It is a delicate subject — for a minister. Other men may talk about it, but not a minister. If he talks about it he is mercenary and worldly minded! But a minister thinks about money. He cannot help it. God has made money a part of his world. He has ordained that money shall play a prominent part in all human life. Clergymen, like other mortals, cannot live without it. It is not disgraceful, therefore, for a minister to earn money and spend it and talk about it. What God has made necessary let no man call unclean. If ministers had discussed church finance more frankly, laymen would now understand it better than they do. Subjects too delicate for discussion gather round them a mass of spontaneous and erroneous opinion. Erroneous opinion concerning matters of moment cripples the church, and blocks the progress of the kingdom.

The salary of the minister is not an alms, but a debt. This is fundamental. Unless a church grasps this, all its after life is bound in shallows and in miseries. A minister is not a beneficiary or a pauper or a beggar. He is a laborer, and the laborer is worthy of his hire. To give him donations and discounts is to demoralize the man and degrade his office. His salary is a debt; and, like all debts, it should be paid fully, promptly, ungrudgingly. A church which holds back a dollar of its pastor's salary is a rogue. If there were a penitentiary for roguish churches it would be full. An honest man's the noblest work of God; a dishonest church is the crowning work of the devil. A minister does wrong in allowing a church to impose upon him. A church which cheats must be disciplined. If, after repeated offences, it refuses to repent, he should shake off the dust of his feet against it.

It is well to pay the minister liberally. A church cannot afford to do otherwise. If church officials drive a hard bargain, and secure a man at the lowest possible figure, they lose more than they gain. A niggardly financial policy will wreck any church. The question should be, not how little shall we pay, but how much? "There is that withholdeth more than is meet, but it tendeth to poverty." Deacons feel mean after they have higgled a week about the pastor's salary. It takes the heart out of a preacher to feel that he is preaching to skinflints.

The average minister is not paid generously. Unless a man is sought after by several churches, his salary is almost sure to be small. If sought after, his salary goes up, not because of Christian liberality, but because of ecclesiastical competition. The average clergyman is underpaid. Often a faithful man works hard for years for small pay, and men of large income in the congregation allow him to do it. But when a call comes from some other church, then the brethren come to their senses, and offer to do what they should have done years before. Such action is contemptible. It should be resented by every minister who has self-respect. No church should offer to advance its minister's salary when he is considering a call to another parish. Such an offer is a bribe. If from a church which has long imposed upon its minister because he was too modest to protest, it comes too late; if from a sudden spasm of enthusiasm the church is stirred to offer more than its resources warrant, its folly should be resisted. A minister's heart is made glad by a people who are generous, not by a people who are shrewd bidders at an auction. A church at all times should pay its pastor up to the level of its ability.

But the chief cause of inadequate salaries is not depravity, but lack of consideration. Laymen are too busy to put themselves in their pastors place, and reason out his needs. There is nothing more amusing than the way the average layman reasons out a minister's "necessary expenses," and calculates the amount he can save. The man in the moon could probably calculate better. A mechanic lives on a certain amount a week. Why should not the minister do the same? Because he is a public character and the mechanic is not. A minister must live in public. He owes duties to the community which it costs money to discharge. He cannot live where he pleases, or dress as pleases, or order his life as he pleases. His position necessitates expenses which other men can escape. His grocer's bill — if he is hospitable — is double that of the average man in his congregation. To preach well he must eat more than beefsteak. He must eat books straight through the year. He should be allowed at least one hundred dollars a year for his library. Thrice or quadruple that amount is not extravagant. To expect a man to preach fresh and juicy sermons while withholding from him nutritious mental food is cruel. A lean library means a scrawny preacher.

A vacation costs money. Many a clergyman stays at home the year round because he cannot afford to take his family out of town; or, if he goes, he preaches in other pulpits every Sunday to pay his travelling and hotel expenses. This is not right. There are a few men, to be sure, who will preach every Sunday during their vacation, no matter what their salary may be; but how is it with your minister? Why does he preach through his vacations?

You cannot know all the channels through which a clergyman's salary trickles away. He owes duties to his denomination; and every council, conference, or convention he attends makes demands upon his purse. You cannot know the cases of need he meets continually, many of which it is impossible to escape. People whose names you would never guess come to him for assistance. In fixing the minister's salary, a generous sum should be added for the express purpose of meeting just such demands. To expose a man to incessant calls for help, and furnish him no funds with which to meet these calls, is an act of short-sightedness as frequent as it is lamentable. Any man worthy to be your pastor may be trusted with a salary liberal enough to enable him to be generous toward the needy individuals and deserving causes which have a reasonable claim upon him as your representative and head. In short, the necessary expenses of a clergyman are unique. His table, his correspondence, his library, his travels, his benevolence, all eat up money with incredible swiftness; and this should be borne in mind when the church discusses the question, "What salary shall we pay?"

XII. Ministerial Liberty

How to secure it is an age-long problem. Arduous efforts have been made to gain it, but success has been only partial. The Roman Catholic Church has made the clergy independent of the laity, but this has not set the clergy free. When men are bound together in a system in which they rise one above another, rank on rank, opportunity is furnished the men above to lord it over the men below. The Catholic priest may pity the Protestant minister because the latter is at the mercy of his fastidious and fickle parishioners, but to be dependent on a congregation for daily bread is not a whit more demoralizing than to be dependent for ecclesiastical preferment on one's ecclesiastical superiors. As a device for gagging men, the hierarchy has proved fatally effective.

The Anglican Church, to escape the tyranny of the pope, has lodged final authority in the state. This is a surrender of the Roman position, and gives supreme power to laymen. But it does not solve the problem. How may clergymen be free? Monarchs and prime ministers are no less formidable than popes and cardinals, and every state church presents to its clergy the temptation of shaping their message to please the men who have political power. In America our Protestant churches, on the whole, vest authority in the people. Majorities, directly or indirectly, rule in church as well as in state. The consequence is, that our churches are exposed to all the dangers and maladies which are inseparable from democracy.

For the people may be as tyrannical as despots and hierarchies. They can degrade the clergyman to a puppet or a parrot. They often do. They can wreck a church whose pastor discredits their opinions, or runs counter to their prejudices. Many a man has been ousted from his pulpit simply because he dared to speak the truth.

How to keep the pulpit independent is one of our greatest problems. It is more than a church problem. It is a question in which every citizen of our republic has a vital interest. It is essential to the life of a republic that it have in it a body of public men free to speak their deepest convictions without fear or favor. We need leaders who are absolutely untrammelled. A large part of the press cannot be relied on. The ledger dictates its policy. It echoes the opinions of the street. It cares nothing for moral leadership, and everything for immense circulation. Many editors are not free men. Neither are many of our political leaders. The exigencies of political warfare render them diplomatic, and compel them to tone down their utterances. They dare not attack evils which ought to be annihilated, or advocate policies which ought to be enthroned. Even college presidents and professors are liable to be called to account by frightened trustees for the utterance of opinions which cut across the grain of popular conviction. In such a land and time it is of sovereign importance that the pulpit should be without a fetter. Its message should be free from every taint of private interest, and from every trace of external constraint. Nothing cuts the ground from under a minister's feet like the suspicion that he is saying, not what he thinks, but what his hearers expect him to say. The church can have no influence over people who believe that clergymen are the hired exponents of the views of the men who rent the pews. The fact that so many clergymen in slavery days apologized for slavery, or winked at it, has done more to bring organized Christianity in this country into disrepute than all the infidel publications of the century.

In wide circles of our people the conviction is deeply rooted that ministers are the slaves of their congregations, repeating a story put into their mouth, afraid to strike established wrongs, or to pass judgment on perfumed sins. And that such pulpit cowards actually exist cannot be denied. The pressure has been too great, and many an unhappy man has fallen.

And what shall be done about it? Some say give us churches generously endowed by the gifts of men who are in their graves, thus making ministers independent of the people to whom they preach. The suggestion is plausible, but hardly wise. The only adequate relief — so it seems to me — is to be found in reconstructed manhood. Not in dead men must we seek salvation, but in men who are alive. The cowards must be driven from the pulpits. Laymen should see that this is done. A man too timid to oppose anything but ancient evils, or condemn anything but distant sins, is too timid to be a herald of the Lord. There should be a healthy sentiment generated in all our churches, making it easier for ministers to speak boldly, and more disgraceful for them to be craven. The preacher should be encouraged to speak out his deepest thought. Lynx-eyed critics, watching for a chance to pounce down upon him for a misstep in the statement of a doctrine, should be converted or excommunicated. Laymen should be large-minded, charitable, and fair. They should not expect the pulpit to reproduce their own ideas, and confirm them in their favorite notions. Oh, for a layman — who has seen him? — large enough to say to his minister at the close of a sermon full of teaching which he cannot accept, "I cannot agree with you now, but I thank you for your sermon. It has done me good, for it has made me think." For a layman to cut down his contribution to the church because the minister has expressed an idea to which he is unable to assent is the act of a man who would bribe a judge — if he dared — to decide in his favor a case in the courts.

But there is no excuse for cowardly ministers. If laymen attempt to intimidate, they, like the devil, should be resisted. Better lose one's pulpit than one's honor. The preacher must do his duty, no matter if it cuts his salary in two. If he is content to mouth the safe opinions of the ruling set in his congregation, he is not a prophet, but a toady. If he is a puppet, manipulated by a few rich men who contribute generously toward church expenses, he deserves the contempt of men, and is sure of the condemnation of God. No mortal on earth is so despicable as a pulpit coward. And the man who stands next to him in the roll of dishonor is a pious despot in the pew.

XIII. Liberty Defined

No, that is not what I meant. Liberty does not mean license. A minister's freedom ends where the rights of his congregation begin. He has no right to say everything in the pulpit that chances to pop into his head. It is not his province to discuss political parties and measures, and harangue people on questions of political economy and physical science. He is a teacher of religion; and if he begins to manifest a sort of omniscience which compels him to expound every species of knowledge, he is unquestionably insane, and should be promptly dismissed.

Nor should he be allowed to preach even the text of the New Testament if his spirit is spiteful and bitter. A preacher is ordained to preach Christ, and no man preaches Christ who is not dominated by the spirit of love. A sermon is full of Christ if it is full of love, though the name of Christ is never mentioned in it; and a sermon, if captious and hateful, is of the devil, even though the name of Jesus opens and closes every paragraph. Laymen have a right to rebel if their minister is not willing to speak the truth in love.

Nor is a clergyman at liberty to preach interpretations of Scripture which overthrow the conceptions of truth for which his pulpit stands in the community. There seems to be lamentable confusion at this point. Every now and then a clergyman appears who feels it to be his inalienable right to preach anything he pleases in any pulpit he is able to get into. If checked in his course he at once poses as a martyr; and the world — which has a strange fondness for martyrs — rends its raiment^ and throws dust on its head, and pours forth its stock denunciations of the ineradicable bigotry and inexpressible depravity of the Christian church. All of which is exceedingly funny, and also pathetic.

Now, the fact is that a man of ordinary discernment and honesty will not attempt to become the pastor of a church whose fundamental doctrines he doubts or denies. To do so is impudence, if not something worse, and deserves the condemnation both of sinners and saints. What right has a Roman Catholic to preach in a Protestant pulpit? and why should a Unitarian desire to smuggle himself into a Trinitarian pastorate? The chasm between Romanism and Protestantism is deep and wide, and so also is the chasm between Trinitarianism and Unitarianism; and nothing is gained by attempting to conceal those chasms. A man is at liberty to make his home in any branch of the Christian church whose creed his mind can accept and his heart rejoice in, but to steal as a teacher into a company of Christians whose basal tenets he discards is the act of a thief and a robber. To cast such a man out of the place which he has usurped is not bigotry or tyranny, but beautiful and necessary justice. There is the widest liberty of religious thought in America; and, with our multiplicity of denominations, there is no reason why any clergyman earnestly desirous of delivering a message should fail to find a congregation willing to grant him all the latitude his soul may desire. It is no infringement of a man's liberty to insist that he stay where he belongs.

But in many churches there are petty tyrannies which ought to be abolished. The pastor of a church is by divine right a leader. As its executive head he is held responsible for the successful administration of its affairs. A man who is held responsible for the conduct of an enterprise must be granted large liberty in the prosecution of his work. A general cannot be condemned for defeat if he is not permitted to lay out his campaign. A business manager who is not allowed to manage is not responsible for the bankruptcy which overtakes his house. A guide who is obliged to follow is no guide at all. A minister is not answerable for the outcome of his ministry if he is thwarted at every step by men who will not approve his methods or adopt and work out his suggestions.

Many a minister is robbed of power by the unreasonable demands of his people. They demand church prosperity, and promptly vote down every measure which is likely to produce it. They lie down in the ruts of outgrown methods, and then berate the poor man who in vain urges them to move forward. They weight him down with the armor of his predecessor, and then stand amazed because he cuts a poor figure in fighting the foe. Every man must work in his own way, and so far as possible the church should endeavor to adjust itself to the temperament and ideas of its leader.

The reluctance to back up the minister, so frequently met with in our churches, is due no doubt in part to the training which laymen receive in the business world. In business they lay down their own plans without advice or interference. They say to one man, "Come," and he comes; to another, "Go," and he goes. Such experience begets in many men a sort of absolutism which works mischief whenever it is introduced into the church. It is easier for a camel to go through the eye of a needle than for men of a certain type to accept graciously outside advice, or to co-operate in the execution of plans forged in the brain of another. The refusal of church-members to subordinate individual wishes and purposes to the working out of a consistent and definite policy has crushed many a minister and wrecked many a church. Jesus himself could do no mighty work among people who had no confidence in him; and unless laymen have sufficient confidence in their pastor to follow him, his ministry must be disappointing to them and disastrous to him. Brethren, if your minister is capable of leading, follow him. If he is incapable, hand him his resignation, and secure his successor. To call a man your leader, and then tie him hand and foot, is action unworthy of sensible men.

But here, again, liberty has its limits. Laymen have a right to help devise as well as to execute. It is not to be expected that they will consent to be automata in the working out of ministerial ideas. If a minister is crotchety or autocratic or bull-headed; if he refuses to take laymen into his counsel; if he insists on having everything his own way, and that, too, before sundown; if he attempts, in short, to be a czar, — he need not be surprised to find some morning that his sceptre is broken and that his throne has passed to another.

XIV. Sympathy

But time and money and liberty are not enough. A minister, like other men, must live by every word that proceedeth out of the mouth of God. And one of God's words is sympathy. By sympathy I do not mean that pinched and insipid thing which the word sympathy oftentimes suggests. Sympathy is more than pity or commiseration. A man does not like to be pitied. Pity suggests inferiority, and easily slides into contempt. "How I do pity ministers!" is a sentimental ejaculation often heard on the lips of persons who know something of the trials which fall to the average parson's lot. But why pity ministers more than other men? Their life is no harder than that of others. Do not all mortals have their drudgeries and bitter cups, their burdens and crowns of thorns? Why should a minister be exempt? Suppose he is gossiped about and maligned, misunderstood and hated? It is enough for the servant that he be as his Master, and the disciple as his Lord. A man who expects to be kept done up in cotton has no business to enter the ministry. He must take up his cross daily, and ought not to whine about it. Constant commiseration is debilitating. Whatever the clergyman's distresses and miseries, he should never be petted or coddled.

But sympathy warms and feeds the heart. It is fellow-feeling. It is feeling in company with another. Every true man needs it. It is tonic. It is life. Without sympathy the minister sickens and starves. The nobler the man, the more dependent he is on human companionship and love. Coarse and callous men are indifferent to environment, but men of fine sensibilities faint and fall unless braced by hearts which love them. There is nothing more pathetic in the Gospels than Jesus' question to the disciples in the Garden of Gethsemane, "Could ye not watch with me one hour?"

The loneliness of the minister — have you ever thought of it? He is one of the most solitary of mortals. He moves among men, but he is isolated from them. Like his Master, he treads the wine-press alone. The world for which he labors is openly hostile or chillingly indifferent. The words are still sadly significant: "Behold I send you forth as sheep in the midst of wolves." The wolves do not use their teeth as they did in the days of the Roman Empire; but teeth they still have, and every minister who does his duty is doomed to be torn to pieces in many a circle of the godless and at many a dinner-table of the Pharisees and the Sadducees. No man can proclaim with unfaltering accent the message written in the New Testament without encountering the vindictive and strenuous opposition of the world. The Sabbath-breakers and the libertines and the rum-sellers, and the gamblers of all stripes and sizes, and the fops and cynics and idlers, will all turn a deaf ear to his teaching, and will either hoot at him, or pass by on the other side in sullen silence. It is a cold and unresponsive world to which the preacher brings his message.

Since, then, the world is unsympathetic, the church should glow with enthusiasm and good-will. Alas! many churches are almost as dead as the world. Laymen in discouraging numbers do not rally round their pastor like brothers round a brother. They, do not feel with him. They consider him an alien. Such laymen are often interested in the social prestige of the church, and take pride in its financial prosperity, but they have no fraternal interest in the man who fills the office of shepherd and teacher. They forget that a minister is human, and needs encouragement and affection. They are good men, but sympathy is not one of their graces.

It is not hostility but indifference which kills preachers. Opposition on the part of obstreperous saints may at times prove medicinal, and prepare a minister for larger work. But apathy — it is fatal. It will take the heart out of a giant. It can discourage even a St. Paul. To plan and hope and toil and pray while all around him professing Christians stand as listless and unconcerned as were the crowds which watched the progress of the awful tragedy on Golgotha, — this is a form of crucifixion which many a minister has suffered, and in many a parish the tragedy still goes on.

Even at the best a minister's work is full of discouragement and disappointment. All that is good and bad in the human heart comes to the surface in a Christian church. One never knows men until he attempts to live with them. Working together in the bonds of church fellowship gives surprising revelations of human nature, and furnishes added proofs of the need of redemption through Christ. Scoffers often grow voluble over the selfishness and hypocrisy inside the churches, but ministers can add several chapters to the scoffers' doleful story. No matter how faithfully a clergyman may labor, he must bear always on his heart the burden of work done apparently in vain. Under his ministry some men degenerate into hypocrites, others fall into open sin, others are carried away by heresies and superstitions. The sword passes through his heart again and again. Because he keeps his despondencies and despairs out of his sermons, do not imagine he has none. There are crises in every minister's life in which a cheering word is meat and drink for forty days. Such words are cups of cold water which considerate laymen will never fail to give.

It is a pernicious heresy that all the church wants of men is their money. No church can live and grow on gold alone. There are other things not a whit less necessary which laymen have it in their power to give, and which they too often thoughtlessly withhold. Just a word of rejoicing when the Spirit works mightily in the parish, and the sterile fields burst into bloom; just a word of regret when the wheels of the Lord's chariot drag heavy and slow — such a word dropped occasionally into the ear of the leader is one of the most valuable contributions which any layman is able to offer. And to offer this is within reach of the humblest. Even the mightiest of the prophets has his strength increased by the whispered "Godspeed" of the poorest and obscurest of God's saints. If the Son of God himself in a darkened hour craved the support of steadfast and sympathetic hearts, be assured that no one of his ministers in these hurried and earthy-hearted times is above the need of the sympathy of his brethren.

XV. Co-operation

But sympathy is not complete until it expresses itself in action. Good feelings are not enough. They must blossom in good deeds. Sympathy without works is dead. Minister and laymen must work together. When they do this, all things are possible. It is because they do not do it that the millennium is so far away.

The curse of the centuries is the delusion that religion is a thing which can be conducted and controlled by the clergy alone. For a thousand years the policy of the Church of Rome fostered this delusion. The entire administration and worship of the church were monopolized by the hierarchy, while the laity degenerated into disfranchised spectators. In many countries this is Catholicism still. One of the sounds which every tourist through Europe brings home with him is the monotonous droning of the priests heard in all the cathedrals and churches. Whether any one is present or not, the industrious repetition of unintelligible words goes on. Christianity seems to be a vast machine whose wheels must be kept everlastingly turning, and whether the turning has any effect on human life or not, it is the business of the clergy to keep the machine grinding. From such foolishness Martin Luther endeavored to deliver Christendom, but three hundred years after his death we have not yet reached the promised land. The virus of the Romish poison is in us still. Errors ingrained by the precept and practice of centuries are not easily eradicated. The luxury of looking on while the priest does the work is too sweet to be surrendered. We count ourselves Protestants, but retain the temper and habits of our Roman Catholic ancestors. In theory we hold that every Christian is a king and priest unto God; that the veil has been rent in twain, giving every follower of Jesus unhindered access to the holy of holies; that to every redeemed soul the command is given, "Go, disciple the nations;" and that all church-members — both laymen and clergymen — are brethren in the Lord. This is our theory, but we shrink from living it.

In many a Protestant parish the minister is practically a priest. To him are committed all the mysteries. His privileges and powers are unique. He must do all the thinking, planning, planting, harvesting. He is responsible for everything that happens, from the conversion of a soul to the creation of a deficit. To him are given the keys of the kingdom of heaven. Whatsoever he binds is bound, and whatsoever he looses is loosed. The church is known by his name. Its own. members have a habit of speaking of it as though they were outsiders. If for any reason prosperity lingers, the fault lies at his door. The laity are spectators. They look on, listen, put money into the contribution-box. This latter makes them bold to do more. They criticise, pass judgment, even crowd into the seat of the scornful. The church is a Sunday theatre, and they take a box for the season. The preacher is the star actor, and the quartet is the orchestra furnishing music between the acts. This is not caricature. It is a photograph — a snap shot taken on the spot — of a section of current Christianity. The photograph may suggest why we have so many distressing and unsolved problems. Until laymen become helpers, yoke-fellows, servants, fellow-laborers, heralds, pastors, fishers of men, co-workers with their leader and with God, the church is, of all institutions, most miserable, and we are yet in our sins.

Is there a church problem which cooperation will not solve? Take, for instance, that of the Sunday evening service. Church-members are rapidly reaching the conclusion that for them one Sunday service is sufficient. Their conviction is also steadfast that the pastor should preach a Sunday evening sermon. The pastor goes into the pulpit, and his people remain in their parlors. The result is a disheartened preacher, and an appalling area of unoccupied pews. This is the Sunday evening problem! How can it be solved? Simply by laymen going to church Sunday evening. Why should they not go? If the need for an evening service has vanished, then by all means let the service be abolished. Each church must determine this for itself. What sense is there in squandering the time of the sexton and the nervous energy of the preacher in keeping up a service the need of which has disappeared? But needed or not, so long as the service is maintained, it is the duty of laymen to attend it.

"We must keep the church open," cry the stay-at-homes, not knowing what they say. When is a church open? When the doors are unbolted and the gas is lighted? No! When a church keeps open house it itself must be present to welcome the guests. An open church means a church with Christians in it ready to welcome all comers. The world cares nothing for empty church buildings. Without people in them they are cold as refrigerators and depressing as sepulchres. A dwindling and deserted church service is one of the deadliest of all enemies of faith. Better hold no service whatever than a service with an occupant in every tenth pew. The Sunday evening service is not attractive unless made so by the Lord's people. Where people in large numbers congregate, other people want to go. It is a cold world, and a fire always draws a crowd. There is no fire so congenial and attractive as that kindled by a large worshipping congregation. To suppose that the unconverted are going to rush into church buildings left vacant by the very men who profess to believe that "he that believeth and is baptized shall be saved; but he that disbelieveth shall be condemned," is to indulge in the suppositions of a fool. A preacher of extraordinary gifts may draw a crowd into a building, but little is gained unless laymen are present to draw the crowd into the kingdom of God. It is not the preacher but the church against which the gates of Hades shall not prevail. When laymen work to fill the churches, preachers will preach better than they do. Every minister ought to have as many assistant pastors as there are members of his church. Unless backed up by his church, he can do nothing. Peter was mighty on the day of Pentecost, not because he had a fluent tongue, but because there stood behind him one hundred and twenty men and women in whose faces there lingered traces of the glory of the tongues of fire.

XVI. Considerateness

It is a high virtue, and a rare one. It involves throwing one's self into another's place. And that takes time. And folks are busy. And that is why there are so many inconsiderate people.

Have you ever made a serious effort to put yourself into a minister's place? Do you realize that he is a public servant, and that a thousand people have a claim upon his strength and time? There are only twenty-four hours in the day, and for every waking hour there are at least a dozen claimants. Evidently a minister cannot do everything which he may be asked to do.

"I wonder where our pastor is. I do not see why he is not here!" petulantly exclaimed one evening in my hearing a leading church woman at a Y. M. C. A. anniversary. She was a saint. She was zealous to have her pastor foremost in every good work and conspicuous in the highest seat at all the feasts. It nettled her to think that he of all men should be absent from an occasion so important. She did not stop to think that a minister cannot attend all the meetings held in his own church, much less those of all the philanthropic and religious organizations which may be doing business in his town. On that very night the supposed culprit was helping forward two other deserving enterprises, one early in the evening by his presence, and the other later on by an address. It is self-evident, and yet needs to be frequently asserted, that a minister cannot be in two places at the same time.

Laymen, as a rule, expect too much; not too much thought in sermons, not too much Christlikeness in character, but too much pottering around at miscellaneous things. In many a parish too much pastoral calling is demanded. There are church-members whose chief end in life, apparently, is to be called upon; and there are clergymen foolish enough to cater to this morbid craving. They coddle the soreheads to reduce their croaking. They steal time from their study to keep people in a good humor who have an abnormal liking for attention. This is all wrong. The chief end of man, or woman, is not receiving pastoral calls; and church-members who grow grumpy if not called upon up to the level of their fancy ought to be excommunicated as disturbers of the peace. There are sins as unchristian and mischievous as drunkenness and prize-fighting, and chronic grumbling is one of them. It is a demon to be cast out of a church at all hazards. No sensible pastor will ever squander time on a professing Christian who has made it the rule of his life not to minister but to be ministered unto, and who compels many to give their lives a ransom for him. Pastoral calling has its place; and a minister who turns his back upon it commits, in my judgment, a serious blunder. Sermons are warmer and juicier after the pastor has been in the homes of his people. There is no book quite so inspiring and suggestive to a genuine preacher as the life of his parish. But pastoral calling may become a millstone round the minister's neck. He may do too much of it. He may wear himself out in the attempt to satisfy the voracious demands of unreasonable people.

Laymen can help the pastor in pastoral work by being considerate. It is not for them to dictate how many calls shall be made each year, or who are the people to be called upon. All such exactions are arbitrary and tyrannical. The pastor knows his parish better than any one else. He knows the people who need him most, knows his own strength and the various demands upon it, and should, therefore, be given large liberty in planning his pastoral labors. To you outsiders the calling may seem haphazard or partial or slovenly, but it will be necessary for you to know a great many things which you do not know now before you are fitted to pass judgment on him. Be considerate. To throw at him as he enters your door the number of months which have elapsed since his last call, or to remind him that some one else has received two calls to your one, or to insinuate that his predecessor was ever so much more faithful in calling than some men you have known, is a species of refined cruelty which Christian love ought to abolish. The only Christian way to get even with the minister, who in your judgment is remiss in coming to see you, is to call upon him yourself. If, as you think, he is doing you an injustice, why not heap coals of fire on his head? Have a quiet talk with him in his study.

Or if you are not brave enough to venture into the parsonage, request him by letter to call on you. If you have a sorrow that you want to talk about, or a sin which you desire to confess, or a problem on which you seek light, send for him. He will be glad to come. It delights a minister to have his people lay their perplexities before him. He is ordained to help people. He cannot help them unless they tell him what it is that troubles them. How much more sensible to invite him into your house, and receive from him the help you need, than to sit and sulk and make the heart bitter by counting up the wrecks which come and go before the door-bell rings. And if you are sick, of course you will send for him. Why not? You send for your physician, why not for your minister? Your physician does not know you are sick unless notified. How can the minister be expected to know? He is a representative of the omniscient God, but he himself has all the limitations of men. The Almighty does not see fit to indicate to his prophets by special revelation the physical condition of the members of the church. When you are sick let the pastor know it. That is sensible, considerate, Christian. But to lie in bed for one week or six, wondering why he doesn't come, telling every caller in plaintive tones that the pastor has not yet called, and to keep on whispering to your friends for six months after you get well that during your illness the pastor never came to see you — that is neither sensible nor considerate nor Christian. Let your considerateness be known unto all men, especially your pastor.

XVII. Thoughtlessness

It causes a deal of mischief in the Church of God. It is not an inhospitable disposition, but thoughtlessness, which leads many church-members to neglect strangers who come to worship with them. Let us hope it is the same distemper which glues men sometimes to the end of their pew, so that late comers are obliged to clamber in over their knees. It is not malice, but heedlessness, which impels a layman to rummage under his pew for overshoes and umbrella during the singing of the closing hymn. What is it but absent-mindedness that starts belated pew-holders up the aisle during the singing of the anthem? Not lack of mind, but lack of thought, is responsible for the conduct of the woman who disturbs her neighbors through prayer and Scripture reading by her incessant whispering. And what but paralysis of the organ of thought can account for the fact that a congregation of courteous people will sometimes turn their back at the close of service upon a minister who has preached in exchange with the pastor without a word of greeting or thanks? To-day, as in the days of Isaiah, the Almighty has just cause to complain, "My people doth not consider."

Thoughtlessness is one of the demons which every minister soon learns to fear. For instance, if some good brother seizes him while on the way to the pulpit, and pours into his ears the latest gossip, it is not considered ministerial to say to such a man, "Get thee behind me, Satan." Though oppressed and afflicted, he must not open his mouth. Or some nervous saint may keep turning over the pages of the hymn-book straight through the preaching of the sermon, not knowing that the constant turning of pages may be to a sensitive man as distracting as the buzzing of a full-fledged sawmill. Or at the close of the service some one may rush forward, and drag him from the pulpit stairs into a subject a thousand miles away from the sermon. This is "the most unkindest cut of all." To labor hard to bring a congregation into the central glory of a truth, and then have some one dash forward at the earliest opportunity — presumptively to render thanks for the help he has received, but in reality to ventilate his mind on some subject totally foreign to the day, or to propound a curious conundrum which has no conceivable relation to anything which has been said — is inexpressibly galling and disheartening. After a preacher has struck with all his might on the heart-chords of a congregation, and then discovers that in at least one of his apparently most attentive listeners there is no hint of a response, he instinctively looks around for Elijah's juniper-tree. Why God allows the devil to play such pranks on ministers in the very hour of their exhaustion is not yet revealed. It may be to bring them more completely into the fellowship of the suffering of his Son. At the close of one of Jesus' sermons on the sin against the Holy Ghost, a preoccupied egotist shouted out, "Master, speak to my brother, that he divide the inheritance with me." It would be hazardous to say that the Son of man ever lost his temper; but if there is a trace of impatience visible anywhere in his recorded sayings, it is in the answer which he gave to this exasperating and incorrigible sinner.

But a dash of cold water at the close of a sermon is not so fatal as an interruption in the midst of sermon-building. It is difficult for the average man to realize the value of uninterrupted time. He himself does not get a day without its interruptions, nor does he want it. A minister, however, if he is to do his best work, must have at least a part of certain days absolutely free from all intrusion. "But I want to see him only a minute," pleads the importunate inquirer, not knowing what he asks. He who thinks that only a minute is a trifle does not know the nature of the mind, and has probably done no sustained and constructive thinking. "Only a minute" may ruin the work of a day. In a minute an express-train can be thrown from the track, but to place it again on the rails requires the arduous labor of hours. The mind in its highest operations moves more swiftly than the limited express, and the interruption of only a minute may hurl the train of thought down an embankment and stop all progress indefinitely. In the hot hours of sermonic creation, when the mental furnace is seething and the molten thought is ready to be poured into words, an outsider who asks for a minute not only checks the momentum of the mental process, but chills the glow of the emotions, and introduces into the mind a foreign substance which is not easily cast out. In those hours when your pastor goes into the mountain to commune with God, do not let the devil tempt you to ring his door-bell.

This seems all foolishness to some of you. You know ministers who are not so cranky. They are open at all times to their people. They say so with swelling pride. Morning, afternoon, and night the latch-string is out, and whosoever will may come. But it must be borne in mind that there are preachers and preachers. Some are carpenters and others are poets. Some men build sermons as carpenters build houses, — they manufacture them. They cut out the material piece by piece, join the pieces together, and sandpaper and varnish them at their leisure. They can drop their work at any moment as easily as the carpenter drops his hammer. The poet-preacher is a different man. His sermons are not made; they grow. Sermons come to him as poems do, in rare and luminous hours, which hours when they come must be seized and used. Some days are opaque. No light streams through. And then there comes —

> One of the charmed days
> When the genius of God doth flow.

Mind and heart are ready. In a few hours the work of weeks bursts into blossom, an argument is forged, a truth is unfolded, a vision is worked out into speech which will make glad many hearts.

As a rule, the preachers who see people at all hours through the week do not see many people at the hour of service on Sunday. If your minister lacks the will-power to protect himself from people who steal his time, you ought to buy him a large-mouthed bulldog, which shall serve as a sort of flaming sword to guard the study door.

XVIII. Ways of Killing a Sermon

A layman may, with a little practice, develop amazing dexterity in counteracting the influence of his pastor. After the preacher has kindled by his sermon a fire in many hearts, a layman may, if industrious and enterprising, extinguish the fire in all the people near him. It is a critical season in the week, — the brief period immediately succeeding the benediction. In those few moments a layman can, if he will, do infinite mischief. He can turn his back on the stranger that stands nearest him, and show by his conduct that the pastor's sermon on Brotherliness is a mere theory, not intended to be reduced to practice, at least in that church. Or, if he chooses to be talkative, he can smother the sermon in his conversation. He can plunge into a discussion of the music. That theme is very fascinating and fatal. He can say: "How did you enjoy the music? How did you like the Soprano?" or, "What did you think of the Bass?" Such questions are exceedingly effective in the mouth of an expert sermon-killer.

A dozen members of the church propounding such questions to every one they meet convert the house of God into a concert-hall, and train people to look upon public worship as a performance to be measured by the aesthetic gratification which it affords to the congregation. Many a minister, after pouring out his very life to convict men of their sins, or to lift them to the level of some arduous duty, has been cut to the heart by hearing his best people discussing in the aisles the excellences or defects of the anthem, and passing judgment on the voices of the singers.

But the question concerning music is not a whit more demoralizing than the question heard even more frequently, "How did you like the sermon?" Asking that question has become a habit which it will probably take centuries to eradicate. It is a demon which can be cast out only by prayer and fasting. Even the saints are addicted to the use of it. When strangers come to the church, the first question at the close of the service often is, "How did you like the sermon?" No wonder spiritual results of preaching are so meagre. What can be expected from preaching unless laymen realize that they are to follow up the work of persuasion by driving home the word set forth by the preacher? Sermons are not toys to be played with, or pretty pieces of rhetoric on which every member of the congregation is expected to pass judgment. To ask, How did you like the sermon? is to drag it down to the level of a crazy-quilt, or a piece of crochet-work. A sermon is not an exquisite bit of literary bric-a-brac, to be chattered over and judged by the technical rules of art. It is not a dumpling into which every self-constituted critic is invited to stick his fork that he may praise or condemn the cook. A sermon is a solemn warning, a bugle-call to duty, a burning condemnation, an earnest stroke against a giant wrong, an exhortation to high endeavor, the illumination of a majestic truth. What a question for an earnest Christian to ask inside the house of God, — "How did you like it?"

Sermons are preached, not to be liked, but to be accepted and lived. Suppose, pray, you did not like the sermon! What of it? Suppose that scapegrace who sat with you in the pew went away disgusted! When the arrow goes in, curses often come out. John the Baptist, Jesus of Nazareth, Peter and John, were not anxious that their sermons should be liked. Why should you be so solicitous concerning the opinion of the critics? Never ask again that insipid question. How did you like the sermon? Such a question injures the one who asks it, and debauches the person who answers it. It trains men to measure sermons by false standards, and to seek for entertainment rather than for truth.

No wonder so many ministers have been spoiled, and are to-day preaching sermons full of everything else but the gospel. They itch to catch the crowd, and cater for applause, because they have been ruined by churches which have trained them to think of the sermon as something to be admired, eulogized, exulted over. A true preacher speaks for God, and whether the people like the message or not is the very last of all questions to be considered. No church can have conversions in it whose leading members ask the unconverted. How did you like the sermon? When a man is wrestling with problems of life and destiny, it is an insult to throw at him such a frivolous inquiry. It calls him off from a decision unspeakably momentous, invites him to pose as a critic, and requests him to pass judgment on the instrument which in the providence of God is being used for his regeneration. Many an aroused soul has been hurled from a serious mood of conviction into the mood of a trifler by, How did you like the sermon?

It is impossible for earnest men to do anything in the pulpit unless they are seconded by earnest men in the pews. Of what avail are passion and solemnity and burning earnestness in the preacher if the sermon is followed up by a swarm of triflers propounding idle questions? Holy impressions are easily dissipated. It does not take much to strangle newborn aspirations. One silly interrogation may crush a rising impulse toward God. The church should carry on and complete the work begun by the preacher. All conversation at the close of the service should deepen and fasten the impression of the hour. The church should be a trumpet through which the voice of the preacher gains volume and power. But if the trumpet gives an uncertain voice, who shall prepare himself for war? If the preacher cries, "In God's name, act!" and the saints stand around and ask, "How do you like that?" who of the unconverted will prepare himself for the marriage supper of the Lamb?

The crucial question is not, Did you like it? but, Did it help you? Did it comfort you? Did it give you new visions of duty? Did it bring you nearer to the Lord? The parable of the sower has an abiding significance. Those birds which devour seeds are like the poor: they are always with us. In our days such birds have no feathers, but in instinct they are true to the nature of the birds which Jesus saw; and one of their favorite methods of rendering vain the work of the Sower is asking. How did you like the sermon?

XIX. Inspiring the Minister

What means the clamor of the churches for young men? It means that youth has vim and passion, and that the gospel has fresh stimulus and tonic on the lips of men whose hearts have not been saddened by disappointment or worn out by burdens too heavy to be borne. He is a rare man who in our day can do the work of a pastor for thirty years and maintain his energy undiminished and his enthusiasm unimpaired. With multiplied experiences to draw the fire out of him, no wonder many a minister becomes in later life as cold as an extinct volcano.

If you wish to keep your minister young, be regular in your church attendance. Possibly a minister ought to rise superior to his environment, and speak with as much unction to quartered oak as to living hearts; but a minister after all is only human, and in the course of time empty pews wear on him. Laymen, as a rule, do not realize the importance of church attendance. If they did they would not so often allow a cloud, or a shower, or a wind, or a snow, or a caller, or a newspaper, or a headache, or a fit of laziness, to keep them at home. A minister deserted by his representative men dies. He dies by inches. No man can preach with sustained fire and hope whose leading people show by their desultory attendance that public worship is to them one of the incidentals or electives of life. Nothing will so surely take the spring and snap out of a man as speaking on great themes to empty pews. It makes a man prematurely old. Brethren, be in your place at the hour for public worship. The church is expected by the world to render worship on the Lord's Day to God. The rendering of this worship is one of the sacrifices to be offered perpetually by the followers of Jesus. The world's redemption is delayed by Christians who mar the sacrifice by selfish neglect to take part in it. Be in your place every time. Your presence gives life to the preacher. Your face helps him more than you can ever know. Your faithfulness strengthens the grip of Christ upon your community, and hastens the coming of the golden age.

And take heed how you hear. Listening is a high art. Among many Christians it is a lost art. Make it your business to pay attention. Whip your mind whenever it runs off. Go after it a hundred times if necessary. Cudgel it back to its work. The church is not a place for lounging or dreaming. Public worship is work; and no one can worship truly unless he girds up the loins of his mind, and makes energetic use of all the intellect and will-power which the Almighty has given him. The failure of intelligent people to take in spoken discourse is something disheartening. He is an exceptional Christian who is able to follow a sermon closely from the first sentence to the last. Hence the ignorance of many church-members. Hence the misunderstandings and misinterpretations. Many persons mishear. Mishearing is chronic with them. They invariably drop out the critical qualifying phrase of a sentence and the cardinal paragraph of a sermon. They do this because their mind takes cat-naps. Like a worn-out sewing-machine, it drops stitches. What minister has not blushed on hearing some of his best listeners endeavor to give a *résumé* of his sermon. Every preacher has reason to be devoutly thankful to God that he is not responsible for everything which people think he has said. It was his insight into human nature which led Christ to end his discourses with, "He that hath ears to hear, let him hear."

Let it not be forgotten that laymen are an important factor in the preaching of a sermon. The sermon is determined by the preacher, the theme, and the congregation. A public speaker, some one has said, gives back in flood what he receives from his audience in vapor. But suppose there is no vapor arising from the people, and that the audience is a Sahara desert, arid and dead. How can a man speak with glowing tongue unless his hearers help him? Preachers in larger numbers will preach with genuine Pentecostal power when their people supply the atmosphere in which great speech becomes possible.

Work, then, for the sermon through the week. You have a part in it as well as your pastor. Subscribe for at least one religious paper that you may keep in touch with the great movements in which God is expressing himself in your time. Buy the best books. Read church history. Study the history of doctrine. Own the great volumes which throw light on the Scriptures. A few men and women in a congregation, informed and truth-hungry, capable of appreciating the best thought which the preacher can give, are a safeguard against ministerial laziness, and a ceaseless spur to more strenuous labor. Such persons call out his reserves and resources. Are you an inspiration to your pastor?

Keep your Sundays free for earnest reading. Burn up the Sunday newspaper. It is an indefensible, intolerable curse. It exists simply and solely to swell the income of wealthy and greedy newspaper proprietors. A Christian ought to be ashamed to have it in his house. Is not a man sufficiently secularized by six days' contact with the world without dipping his mind on Sunday morning once more into the muddy stream in which he has dipped it on the preceding six days? What can be expected of a Christian in public worship who comes to church with a newspaper stuffed into his mind? He is cold as a clod to the touch of the preacher, and lowers the spiritual temperature of the entire congregation. William E. Gladstone was an ideal worshipper in God's house. He concentrated all his great powers upon the sermon. He was interested because he was informed. He was informed because throughout life he had made diligent use of his Sundays. He declared in old age that he would not have lived so long had he not always kept his Sundays quite apart from his political life. It was pure refreshment to him to turn to holier things on that day. It enabled him to learn more of religious subjects than perhaps any other layman of our century. It gave him that firm and splendid ground which ennobled and hallowed all his actions. "Go thou and do likewise."

XX. Appreciating the Minister

Ministers are human. They have hands, organs, dimensions, senses, affections, passions. If you prick them they bleed, and if you appreciate them they are strengthened. They are more sensitive to appreciation than most men because of the nature of their work. Their work is heart work. It is arduous and exhausting. It involves their sympathies and affections. To have a thankless congregation is an agony something like that of having a thankless child.

Moreover, a minister has many things to worry him. He is subject to constant and merciless criticism. He is never eager to hear all the things that people are saying, but in the course of the year he is certain to catch enough of the tittle-tattle which goes on around him to trouble and depress him. In this way anxieties and suspicions often arise which faith is not able to shake off. The flippant remark of some petulant critic may lie like lead on his heart for weeks. He loses confidence in himself. He imagines his critics more numerous than they are. It has happened more than once that a good man has been worried into insanity, or the grave, by the impression that his parish was hostile to him. The impression may have been created by the bad feeling known to exist in only two or three homes. A minister, to do his best work, must live in an atmosphere of good will. Laymen ought to create such an atmosphere. While the busybodies are carrying to the pastor stories of dissatisfaction, the saints ought to bear to him messages of affectionate good cheer and enthusiastic approval.

The finest results of a minister's labors are below the reach of the eye. They cannot be computed or tabulated. They are spiritual satisfactions, heart impulsions, soul inspirations, which only those who receive them know anything about. A minister often fails to realize the magnitude of the work he is doing. Because the people say nothing, he concludes his ministry is in vain. Many a clergyman has carried a burdened heart through years of disappointing labor, hungry for a word of appreciation which never came, finally throwing down his work in despair, only to find on the eve of his departure to another parish or the other world, how wide was the satisfaction, and how genuine the affection for him in the hearts of the people. Just a word of commendation now and then through the silent years would have brightened many a day that was dark, and made lighter many a burden which almost crushed. Tell your minister, brethren, that you appreciate what he is doing. Praise, like mercy, is twice blessed. It blesses those who give as well as those who receive. It is a shameful thing to sit for a year under preaching which makes you a nobler and happier man without letting your pastor know that in at least one heart the seed has fallen, and is bringing forth many fold.

Laymen ought to practise Paul's words: "I praise you." Why not praise your pastor? Are you afraid of spoiling him? Do not fear. Praise spoils no one who is not spoiled already. It is true, as Wordsworth says, that "Praise is dangerous." But so also is every other good thing. For every man hurt by praise, a thousand are starved to death by lack of it. There is nothing which humbles a true man like generous appreciation.

Many persons are so unaccustomed to speak complimentary words that when they attempt it, the words stick in their throat; or if the words get out, they are badly bungled. No man under thirty can be told that his sermon is very good for a young man, without resenting it. He has Paul's authority for refusing to allow men to despise his youth. It is galling to a man over sixty to receive compliments with a reference to his age tacked away in one end of them — a sting, as it were, in their tail. Nor is it edifying to hear a person begin with, "I don't want to flatter you, but" — Such a remark is equivalent to saying, "Please don't think I'm a liar because I say I enjoyed your discourse." Nor does a sensible man want to be assured that his sermon was "grand," or that his prayer was "splendid." Such encomiums are almost as bad as the eulogy of the brother who invariably prefaces his remarks with a declaration that he believes it to be his duty to encourage a man when he does well. Grown men do not like to be patted patronizingly on the head. Words of commendation, when squeezed through the lips by a hard sense of duty, bring a chill, instead of a glow, to the heart. Praise is best when it comes easily and naturally, —

"As showers from the clouds of summer.
Or tears from the eyelids start."

A quiet, "I thank you for your prayer," or "Your sermon helped me," is worth more than all the stilted English which a voluble enthusiast is able to pour into a preacher's ears.

There are ministers who seldom receive a word of praise. Their big, eloquent brothers go through life with hosannas ringing perpetually in their ears, while they drudge on unnoticed, with no one to stir their pulses by shouting, "Well done." It is a mistake to suppose that God's commendation alone is sufficient. Moses was strong, but he was not strong enough to hold up his hands to the end of the day. "Aaron and Hur stayed up his hands, the one on the one side and the other on the other side, and his hands were steady until the going down of the sun." Happy the minister who is steadied and sustained by Christians who appreciate the work that is being done, and who hearten their leader by a frequent word of gratitude and appreciation. A minister was one day surprised at the close of his sermon to have a stranger greet him thus: "I thank you for that sermon; it did me good." He had preached faithfully for a year, and no member of his congregation had in all that time expressed to him a word of appreciation. The words of the stranger overcame him. To be assured that a sermon of his had reached the heart was like rain on thirsty soil. He hurried home and told his wife the good news. They bowed their heads and wept together.

XXI. Criticising the Minister

It is a difficult task, but there are times when it must be done. By criticism I do not mean that aimless detraction in which undeveloped church-members occasionally indulge, but the brave and open disapprobation of a minister's conduct, or the condemning judgment of his work. Ministers are not infallible. Like other mortals, they fall into ruts. They sometimes allow idiosyncrasies to become so pronounced as to narrow their influence and cripple their power. Alas for a man who is placed beyond the reach of intelligent and discriminating criticism! There is scarcely any limit to the number of foolish things a minister may be guilty of. He may come to church meetings habitually late, or he may sniffle at the close of every paragraph, or he may whoop like a wild Indian in delivering tame ideas, or he may practise elocutionary slides in his prayers, or he may make faces which frighten the children, or he may stare at the wall instead of looking at the people while preaching his sermons, or he may make the church a place in which to rehearse the chapters of his next book, or he may refer in every sermon to his trip to the Holy Land, or he may make Missions or some other equally good theme his hobby, and ride it straight through the year, or he may allow his voice to drop into inaudibility at the close of every important sentence, or he may repeat old sermons so frequently that even people with a poor memory find him out, or he may go gadding over the country shining at all sorts of celebrations while his people sit in darkness at home, or he may keep on for years mispronouncing a half-dozen common words to the disgust of every high-school girl in the congregation, or — What does your minister do? "Oh, if he would only quit that!" is the distressed cry of many a long-suffering saint who wants to cure his pastor of a bad habit, and does not know how to go about it.

What can be done? The providential remedy is a wife, but the remedy is not always sufficient. Some men do not marry, and some wives do not know how to criticise. Some women are adepts in criticism; but their husbands, being stiff-necked and rebellious, refuse to hearken to their strictures and admonitions. It is not uncommon for both the minister and his wife to tumble into the same ditch. What can you do? Will you write him an anonymous letter? Never! It is the work of a coward and a sneak. A minister who values his time will not read anonymous letters. Life is too short to waste it in reading communications whose writers are ashamed to own them. If a minister is foolish enough to read an anonymous, faultfinding letter, he is almost sure to think it the production of some crank or knave, and consequently its appeal does not lead him to repentance. Do not write such letters. If you know something you are convinced that your pastor ought to know, stand up and say it to him like a man. "I withstood him to the face," says Paul, in describing the way in which he rebuked Peter. Paul knew how to censure as well as how to praise.

The object of Christian criticism is to edify. To edify is to build up. A man is not built up by criticism which he never hears. Consequently it is foolish to criticise a minister behind his back. Such disparagement may offer an outlet for one's bad humor, but it does not redound to the glory of God.

If the talk is carried on in the presence of children, it becomes a tenfold greater sin. What deeper wound can a parent inflict upon his child than to render the minister of religion ridiculous to him by laughing at his mannerisms, or depreciating his intelligence or his piety! Children are easily prejudiced, and their hearts can be readily closed. They are naturally trustful and receptive, their affections are fresh, and their confidence in adults is unbounded. They give their hearts readily to those who are placed over them, and it is in their docility of heart that there lies the possibility of education and culture. To criticise in their presence those whose business it is to mould them, destroys in them the very capacity which it is the duty of parents to safeguard and develop. The more deeply a child loves his pastor or teacher, the more he will learn from him. How can a boy be helped by a minister whom his father picks to pieces every Sunday? How can the life of a girl be moulded by a man whose methods and attainments are constantly sneered at by her mother? Many parents have lamented in later life that their children did not join the church, not knowing how to account for such conduct, when the reason was that the children lost confidence in the church on account of the conversations they heard at the dinner-table. No matter how limited in wisdom or goodness the minister may be, it is wicked to criticise him in the presence of boys and girls. The office of the minister of Christ is sacred, and the child-heart should be trained to reverence the office by being taught to honor the man who fills it.

Whenever, therefore, you want to censure your pastor, follow the directions given by the Lord in the eighteenth chapter of St. Matthew's Gospel. The minister is your brother, and if he has trespassed against you by actions which offend, go and tell him his fault between you and him alone. If he is willing to hear you, you have done both him and the church an invaluable service. But if he will not hear you, then take with you one or two more, that he may know your criticism is not a personal crotchet, but the sober judgment of representative members of the church. If he shall neglect to hear them, tell it unto the church. A minister too touchy and stubborn to listen to the counsel of his best people is a fit subject for church discipline. If he insists on acting like a heathen, he ought to be treated like one. Many a clergyman has injured his influence for years by some oddity of behavior or crudity of character which might have been corrected in a day had a few sane and substantial laymen been brave enough to call his attention to the thing wherein he gave offence.

XXII. Securing a Minister

There is only one thing more difficult, and that is getting rid of one. In saying this, I take it for granted that you are under a democratic form of church government. If your church is a monarchy, the problem is a simple one. In that case the preacher is ordered to his post by his superior officer. The congregation has nothing to say. The preacher is sent. The church accepts him.

But Christians in increasing numbers are insisting on the right to say who shall be their spiritual leaders. Even in churches whose government is monarchical, there is a growing disposition among the laity to transfer the appointment of the clergyman from the hands of the hierarchy into the hands of the congregation. It is a privilege highly prized, but for it Christendom is paying a great price. If monarchy has its dangers and tyrannies, so also has democracy its limitations and madnesses. When the local church is officered by external authority, there is often friction, and sometimes open rebellion. When the local church is left to select its own leader, there is often a storm at his coming, and a battle over his departure.

One of the first steps to be taken in the needed reform is to abolish the ancient and pernicious custom of candidating. It is a device of Satan for humiliating ministers and dividing churches. The system is plausible, and ingenious arguments can be made for it. But "there is a way which seemeth right unto a man, but the end thereof are the ways of death." A minister preaches as a candidate. His voice and gestures, his necktie and theology, his coat and rhetoric, — all come under severe scrutiny. At the close of the sermon a canvass is made to ascertain what the popular estimate of the man is. There are usually a few who have heard of another son of thunder who looms up as a possible prize, and this man must of course be heard before the vote is taken. He preaches, and the church is immediately divided. A congregation of intelligent people cannot be expected to agree in their tastes. Preachers differ from one another as widely as fruits do. Some people like apples best, others prefer peaches, others plums, others pears, and others grapes. There is no use arguing about tastes. As with fruits, so with men. One man prefers Shakespeare, another Milton, another Burns. There is no use trying to persuade them to agree. Whenever two preachers of equal ability are placed in competition before a congregation, a division is inevitable. The amazing thing is that so many laymen do not see this. After the church has been split into two factions, it is customary to hear a third candidate, which usually results in the creation of a third faction. This leads to a fourth candidate and an additional faction. Multitudes of churches have taken this broad road which leads to destruction, and other multitudes are rushing on to wreck themselves by indulging in the same inexcusable folly.

If a candidate is heard at all, every wise man in the church should strenuously insist on a vote being taken before another man is allowed to go into the pulpit. The candidate himself should demand this. If a church is unwilling to grant his request, then he should pass by on the other side. Such a church is too willful and foolish to deserve a sensible man for its leader.

The best advice to a church is. Candidate not at all. It is a useless piece of business at the best. What can you tell from one sermon? A shallow man, confident and magnetic, may please you at first hearing, while a worthy man, from humility or physical trepidation, may disappoint you. You must hear a man preach for a year before you have a right to judge him. Good preachers are better in their twentieth sermon than in their first. Candidating does not tell you enough. A minister is more than a preacher. He does various kinds of work. Fidelity in these other labors is as important as ability in pulpit ministration. Manhood is the supreme qualification. You cannot judge of manhood in one sermon.

Candidating is a disgrace to the house of God. Who thinks of God when a candidate is preaching? Not the preacher, because he is thinking of the people; not the people, because they are dissecting the preacher. Nothing is so demoralizing to a Christian church as candidating. It converts public worship into a farce.

Moreover, it is humiliating to the preacher. To be inspected like a pumpkin at a fair, to be put through the paces like a horse at a race, to be judged by a miscellaneous assembly many of whom do not know what a good sermon is, is an outrage upon clergymen which ought to be abolished forthwith.

But how shall a church know whom to choose? Let it choose a man on his record. A clergyman is an epistle known and read of all men. He does not do his work in a corner. Fidelity in one field is a better recommendation than a dozen sermons preached on exhibition. If certain brethren feel unable to vote for a man whom they have not seen and handled, let them hear that man in his own church. It is their duty to travel to him, and not his duty to come to them. But suppose the preacher is just out of school? Let him be called on his record as a student and a man. We shall have a new consecration among ministers when it is once fully understood that a man is called on his record. But a church might be disappointed! Of course it might. The chances for disappointment, however, are not so many as under the present system. Many a man who goes up like a rocket in his first sermon, comes down like a stick in his tenth. Hundreds of churches suffer to-day under the ministry of men who were chosen on the impulse of first impressions, rather than on the record of faithful and successful work.

This is no new theory. It has been acted on again and again. Many leading pulpits are now filled by men who were called to their places without preaching as candidates. As a rule, it is the little churches which are most fussy and fastidious, and are capable of greatest tyranny and folly. Every church which by its action registers its disapproval of the custom of candidating, does an invaluable service, not only to the clergy, but to the entire Christian world.

XXIII. Dismissing a Minister

If all ministers had the ability to sense a situation, there would be less tribulation among the saints. But alas! some of the best of men are the stupidest in discerning the signs of the times. Some times it is not blindness, but a wrong philosophy which causes the trouble. The minister sees that he is not the man for the place, but he hangs on under the impression that hanging on is one of the rights delivered once for all to the apostles and their successors. Some clergymen start out wrong, and they stay wrong to the end. They place themselves first, and the church second. Any minister who does that is fated to cause mischief. If a man in the ministry is unwilling to sacrifice himself for the good of the church, he is a dangerous man. Beware of him! There are men who all the way through argue every church question from the ministerial standpoint. "I ought to receive so much salary — therefore!" — It is just such an argument which accounts for hundreds of ministerial loafers. They never get a pulpit, because the salary never reaches their standard. "I have a majority of the people with me — therefore!" — A man who so argues has a devil in him, and is sure to split a church. "I have my children to educate — therefore!" — As though the chief end of a clergyman is to send his children through college. "I have preached here many years — therefore!" — That is a pillow on which many a worn-out herald of the cross is sleeping. When ministers are the slaves of false logic, the only relief is to be found in the laity. It is the duty of laymen to safeguard the interests of the church, and they must do this, though the doing of it costs them sacrifice and causes good men pain. The long-suffering patience of church-members under pastors who are intellectually or temperamentally or physically unfit for their position, is indescribably pathetic. To be sure there are here and there crotchety and fickle churches which have no mercy on ministers; but for every such church there are a score of churches which are willing to bear to the uttermost with a minister whose ministry is a long-drawn affliction.

The forbearance, however, is often the product of necessity rather than of grace. In sheer helplessness the people submit to a scourge which they know not how to escape. What is more pitiable than the predicament of a church with a minister who ought to resign and who does not have the grace to do it? The usual method is to allow things to drag on until both sides are worn out. An immense amount of growling is done behind the minister's back, but of square, manly action there is little. Sometimes a slight cut in the salary is given as a hint. Sometimes the hint takes the form of irregular church attendance. But all such methods of beating around the bush are unbecoming to Christian men.

Laymen should not hesitate to exercise their rights. If a minister is not intellectually strong enough to lead a parish he ought to resign. If he does not resign of his own accord, he should be requested to do it. What right has a minister unequal to his task to wreck a church simply because the church, in ignorance of his ability, once gave him a call? Or if he has crossed the dead line, he should be promptly retired. Some men cross it early. Some men never cross it. Age has nothing to do with it. A man crosses it whenever he ceases to study. No man who is not a student should be allowed to remain in a Christian pulpit. It is a burning disgrace that so many laymen are indifferent at this point. They allow their pastor to dawdle away his time without protest. It is the duty of a layman to be up and after a minister who commits the unpardonable sin of starving his church. Any minister who, ordained to preach the gospel, goes into the pulpit Sunday after Sunday to rehash a few stale exhortations or retail a half-dozen insipid anecdotes, ought to be driven out of the pulpit by laymen burning with the same fiery indignation which led the Son of God to hurl thunderbolts at the men who sat in Moses' seat.

It is not true, as is sometimes taken for granted, that a minister has a right to hold his pulpit until he dies. His term of office is measured by the duration of his ability to perform efficiently the duties of his ministry. The progress of the kingdom of God has been lamentably delayed by the obstinacy of clergymen who have held on to their places long years after their usefulness had ceased. What sadder spectacle can there be than a church gradually disintegrating, its congregations dwindling, its Sunday-school shrivelling, its young people scattering, its finances shrinking, its influence dying, and all because the good man in the pulpit cannot see that the hour for his departure is at hand. The hoary head is a crown of glory if it be found in the way of righteousness, but when the gray-headed man is so unrighteous as to be willing to kill a church rather than have an assistant or get out of the way, he ought to receive the rebuke which his selfishness deserves. The fact that in his prime he did valiant service is not sufficient reason for his retention. Why rob one generation by foisting upon it a man who wore himself out serving the generation preceding?

Nor ought his limited bank account to be a controlling factor in determining the policy of the church. What an outrage, to stunt and starve the spiritual life of a community because the minister needs a living! Every church should pay its minister so generously that ample provision can be made for old age. A few hundred dollars added each year to his salary to pay for an endowment life insurance policy would take away the necessity of keeping him in the pulpit after his pulpit power has vanished. Courage and frankness then are of sovereign importance. Church officials should express to their pastor their deepest convictions. Many a minister has been allowed by his most intimate friends to go on in utter ignorance of the rising feeling against him, suffering at last needless and unspeakably bitter humiliations, simply because his brothers in Christ were too timid and tender-hearted to do their duty.

XXIV. The Minister's Wife

I knew you would want to talk about her — people always do. I do not blame you. I cannot refrain from saying a word about her myself. Since a man and his wife are one, no revelation of a minister would be complete which ignored or slighted the mistress of the manse.

Yes, she has a hard time, but not so hard as some of you imagine. Her tribulations have been greatly overestimated. When she has a harder time than other women, it is frequently her own fault. A parson's wife has unique opportunities for blundering. When such opportunities are numberless, it is a rare woman who is able to turn her back upon them all. Many a minister's wife makes herself wretched by attempting the impossible. It is impossible, for instance, to please everybody; and woe to the mortal foolish enough to attempt it. The chief end of woman is not to please people, but to do her duty. A failure to learn this has wrecked the happiness of many hearts. Or she may attempt to keep pace with her husband in pastoral calling. A woman who takes upon herself the pastoral work of a large parish need not be surprised to find herself, sooner or later, in a nervine hospital. God punishes women who break his law in a foolish ambition to satisfy public expectations. Or she may try to walk in the footsteps of her predecessor. This is a gratuitous method of self-immolation. No two women have the same nature, and it is foolish to wear one's self out in trying to do things simply because somebody else did them. Or she may allow the good women of the parish to place her on the twelve thrones of Israel — a proceeding which invariably invites disaster. Uneasy lies the head that wears twelve crowns! It is much better, as a rule, for a minister's wife to let other women sit on the thrones, while she takes her place among the loyal workers who engage in obscure and unofficial labors. Because a woman is married to a minister, it does not follow that she must be the president of every organization in the parish, or preside at every public meeting which women may hold. No minister's wife should bear any more parish burdens than her own good sense tells her she ought to carry. To carry them simply because some good and officious sister thinks she ought to do it is consummate foolishness.

Much depends upon the way a minister's wife uses her tongue. It is not necessary for her to talk about her ideas of what a church has a right to expect of her. People will find out her ideas from her conduct. Ministers frequently start antagonisms on entering a parish by blowing a trumpet at the gate announcing to the faithful what they propose to do. If they would quietly do what they propose to do, and say nothing about it, there would be less friction and more progress. A minister's wife who blows a trumpet on entering the town, publishing what she will do and what she will not do, inevitably stirs up oppositions which she will never be able to overcome. If she intends to perform marvellous feats, her intention should be kept a profound secret; if she proposes to shake off most of the burdens which the wives of clergymen usually carry, she should be exceedingly meek and say nothing. The people of a parish will allow a minister's wife to do practically what she pleases, if she does not challenge their criticism by shouting from the housetop what she considers her privileges and rights. It is remarkable how sensible most Christians are if they are not provoked to act the fool. Just a spark of folly in the pastor or his wife will often kindle a conflagration of foolishness which no one can extinguish. Whenever you hear a clergyman or his wife laying down in public the limits of their obligations and the extent of their duties, look out for a squall. If a minister and his wife offend not in tongue, the same are a perfect couple.

But the minister's wife is not always to blame. There are women in every parish who are adepts in the art of making the wife of the minister uncomfortable. They can call on her at all hours of the day, upsetting her plans and interrupting her work. They can everlastingly urge her to call on them. If she accepted every invitation to call, there would be no time left for anything else. They can repeat to her all the dismal stories afloat in the parish. They can insist upon her taking the leadership in every good cause, whether God created her for leadership or not. They can give her advice without being asked for it. They can say uncharitable things, and make damaging comparisons, and — it would take a woman to enumerate all the things which women can do.

Let her alone. If she has children, and wants to stay at home with them, let her do it. It is her right to do it. If she prefers to give her time to her husband, helping him in his correspondence, and bearing the burden of household cares, let her do it. There are other kinds of Christian work besides work done at sewing-bees and missionary meetings. It is work enough for any woman, just taking care of a minister. If she is timid and retiring, let her alone. What right have you to haul her out in public places when every fibre of her being revolts against it? If she wants to dress plainly or superbly, let her alone. If her husband is satisfied, you ought to be. If, on the other hand, she insists on running everything, — from her own kitchen up to the missionary convention, — forgive her. Some women are made that way; they cannot help it. If she has an unbridled tongue, and persists in saying things which ought to be left unsaid, do not repeat them. A woman who rehearses through the parish the foolish remarks of injudicious women is more blameworthy than the women who first spoke them. If she has poor taste in dress, and slight tact in conversation, and scant ability in housekeeping, you, cannot cure her by talking. Minister's wives are very much like their husbands, — they are not perfect. They could, no doubt, have been created perfect, but God made them to match the men. It is not to be expected a woman should be your ideal minister's wife. It is sufficient that she be the ideal of her husband.

XXV. The Mission of Laymen

The New Testament likes laymen. It knows nothing of that unique dignity and supernatural authority of the clergy which have been the curse of the Christian world. The church on the day of Pentecost was a democracy. From the days of Moses onward the deepest wish of Israel had been, "Would God that all the Lord's people were prophets, that the Lord would put his spirit upon them." Prophecy at its highest had dared to say that such a time was coming. Peter in his opening sermon declared that the dreams and prophecies of the ages were at last fulfilled. God had indeed poured out his spirit upon all flesh, — upon women as well as men, upon the young as well as upon the old. All were prophets. All spoke for God. Upon each head there sat a tongue of fire. They were all filled with the Holy Ghost. The greatest word m the Book of the Acts is "All." *All* were baptized; *all* spoke; *all* prayed; *all* spread abroad the good tidings; *all* participated in public worship; *all* exercised authority in church government; *all* were thrilled by the rapture of a great love, ennobled by the weight of a great responsibility, and zealous in the performance of a great task. The apostolic church was mighty because it was a brotherhood, and all believers had all things common.

But into this new Garden of Eden a serpent crawled, — ecclesiastical ambition. By slow advances the clergy encroached upon the rights of the laity, crowding laymen from the position given them by the Lord. The Church of God ceased to be a brotherhood. It became a monarchy, with rulers and subjects. All authority passed little by little into the hands of the clergy. With the growth of the hierarchy the power and the glory of the church of the apostles vanished. The dark ages were the ages in which the hierarchy was supreme.

The Reformation in the sixteenth century was a triumph of laymen. Martin Luther could have done nothing had it not been for the laity of Germany. In England the head of the Reformation was a layman. It was largely by the energy of laymen that the English Church was reconstructed; and it was by the laymen of Cromwell's army that the Stuart despotism was crushed, and the history of political liberty was opened. The great event of the sixteenth century was the rise of the laity in the Christian church. Modern history began when the laity resumed their rightful place in public worship. For a thousand years they had simply assisted at rites wrought for them by priestly hands. A new day dawned when "the people were called into the chancel," and public worship became a common prayer of the whole body of worshippers. The Book of Common Prayer is the monument of an immortal triumph. As soon as the Mass, which is a sacrifice wrought through priestly intervention, was superseded by the "communion service," laymen once more enjoyed the privilege which belonged to them in apostolic days, and tasted anew the blessedness of Christian fellowship. The stream of centuries was turned out of its channel by allowing laymen their New-Testament rights as worshippers.

But the world awaits a new reformation. The church to-day is not yet apostolic. It limps and halts. In the midst of vast opportunities it stands impotent and bewildered. Hundreds of ministers are sick at heart. Many of them have grown pessimistic. Occasionally one of them drifts into infidelity. The majority of them are discouraged. It would be a revelation to the world should clergymen speak out plainly what they know and suffer.

We shall never get out of the ditch until laymen realize that they also are successors of the apostles. They stand in the line of a great succession. They are called to be kings and priests unto God. The trouble now is that laymen in large numbers are not in the church. Their names are in the church book, but they themselves are not in the church. Some of them are in their business, and others in their lodge, but too few of them are in the church. No man is in the church whose heart and mind are not in it. The church is hungering for the thought and affection of her men. There is enough brain-power in every church to solve all its problems if this brain-power were utilized. The problems will never be settled so long as men think that paying their pew-rent satisfies all the legitimate claims which organized Christianity makes upon them. The great need of the church is not money, but life. With new volumes of mental and spiritual energy, money would flow in like a mighty stream. Laymen have won their rights as worshippers, they have not yet accepted their privileges as workers. This is the next step in the world's redemption.

According to the New Testament every Christian is a herald, a pastor, a missionary. Every follower of Christ is ordered into the vineyard. Unless he takes up his cross daily, he does not belong to Christ. But this is a page of the New Testament little heeded. "The fields are white unto the harvest, but the laborers are few." The minister goes into the field, and the majority of his people go somewhere else. This, in a sentence, is the running sore of Christendom. Why are churches half empty? Laymen do not work to fill them. Why are deficits so universal? Laymen do not plan to abolish them. Why does the church make so few converts? Laymen do not talk on the subject of religion. Why does church life flow in such feeble streams? Laymen do not pour their life into it.

The baptism for which the church is waiting is the baptism of larger knowledge. We do not seem to know the things which belong unto peace.

They are hid from our eyes. We do not comprehend what this means: "One is your Master, and all ye are brethren." We stumble over this: "As my Father hath sent me, even so send I you." We forget to whom this is spoken: "Go and make disciples of all the nations." We cannot say with Paul: "I rejoice in my sufferings, and fill up on my part that which is lacking of the afflictions of Christ," because we do not realize that we, laymen as well as clergymen, are called to be "laborers together with God." And yet, "It is a faithful saying: For if we be dead with him, we shall also live with him. If we suffer, we shall also reign with him."

www.ingramcontent.com/pod-product-compliance
Lightning Source LLC
Chambersburg PA
CBHW020021050426
42450CB00005B/575